The
British
Motor Bus

A magnificent selection of coaches gathers at Cheltenham coach station — the 'Charing Cross of the Coachways' — in 1934. The most prominent vehicles include a Daimler CF6 of Allchin, Northampton, a Bristol B of Bristol Tramways, a Leyland Tiger of Wilts & Dorset, an AEC Regal of Royal Blue, a Daimler CF6 of Liberty, Cardiff, and a Maudslay ML4 of South London Coaches.

The British Motor Bus

An Illustrated History
by Gavin Booth

LONDON

IAN ALLAN LTD

First published 1977

ISBN 0 7110 0817 5

© Gavin Booth 1977

Published by Ian Allan Ltd, Shepperton, Surrey,
and printed in the United Kingdom by
Ian Allan Printing Ltd.

The side-engined AEC Q was one
of the most unusual and advanced
models to go into production in
the 1930s. This fine 1935 example
was in the fleet of the Aylesbury
independent Keith Coaches.

Contents

Acknowledgements

Gathering a representative selection of photographs is never easy for a book such as this. Unpublished photos, particularly of older vehicles, are notoriously difficult to find, but I have endeavoured to strike a balance between familiar and less familiar views.

The photo credits, where known, are listed below, and I should like to acknowledge my thanks to the individuals and organisations named, for the willing help they gave me. I am particularly grateful to several gentlemen who went to a great deal of extra trouble to supply photographs and to provide and check information; they are John Parke, editor of *Buses*, John Aldridge, deputy editor of *Motor Transport*, Doug Jack of Leyland Truck and Bus, T. W. Moore and Jasper Pettie.

AEC: 5, 41, 43, 44, 45, 47 (upper), 58, 64 (upper), 73 (centre and bottom), 85, 89, 91 (upper).
H. F. Adcock: 55 (centre), 59 (upper).
Ian Allan Library: 2/3, 18 (upper), 20, 25, 29 (lower), 34 (upper), 37, 39 (centre), 48 (bottom), 49 (upper), 50, 51 (upper), 55 (bottom), 60, 62, 63 (upper), 65, 66, 68, 69, 71, 76, 77, 79, 80, 86, 92 (upper).
John Aldridge: 81 (upper), 93 (centre).
Bedford: 53 (lower), 73 (top), 90, 101 (top).
Gavin Booth: Jacket, 40 (upper), 94 (upper), 105 (bottom), 109 (bottom).
Gavin Booth Collection: 13 (upper), 17, 26, 32 (upper), 35, 42, 46, 47 (lower), 52 (top), 55 (top left), 56 (lower), 59 (lower), 61, 63 (lower), 67, 102, 104.
British Leyland Truck and Bus: 98 (upper), 99 (upper), 101 (bottom), 105 (top and centre), 111.
British Rail (Western Region): 9, 16, 49 (lower).
Bus and Coach: 13 (lower), 40 (lower).
Daimler: 21, 24.
Duple: 54, 84.
Ford: 101 (centre).
Greater Manchester PTE: 107 (lower).
Leyland: 15, 23, 29 (upper), 53 (upper), 57, 74, 78, 82, 92 (lower).
London Country: 95.
London Transport: 11, 14, 18 (lower), 19, 27, 34 (lower), 36, 39 (top), 55 (top right), 91 (lower).
Lothian Region Transport: 12, 33.
T. W. Moore: 70, 72, 83, 87, 88, 94 (lower), 96, 97 (upper), 100, 106, 110 (bottom).
T. W. Moore Collection: 56 (upper), 64 (lower).
National Benzole: 93 (top).
National Bus Company: 98 (lower), 109 (top), 110 (centre).
A. J. Owen: 48 (top and centre), 52 (centre and bottom).
M. A. Penn: 81 (lower).
Ribble Enthusiasts' Club: 51 (lower).
Scottish Bus Group: 8, 22 (upper), 30, 31, 32 (lower), 97 (lower).
Scottish Postal Board: 110 (top).
Edward Shirras: 93 (bottom).
M. J. Tozer Collection: 22 (lower).
Trent Motor Traction: 28, 38.
Tyne & Wear PTE: 108.
Volvo: 99 (lower), 103.
R. L Wilson: 107 (upper).
R. L. Wilson Collection: 39 (bottom).

Foreword

One of the first things any writer discovers when researching a book such as this is that historians often disagree in the way they record or interpret important events. This has certainly been my experience. Time has an irritating way of clouding precise memories, so where there was any doubt I have included my own interpretation of various events. Then there is the further danger of distortion, for a number of the available bus books have been primarily public relations exercises written for the greater glorification of the operator or manufacturer concerned. But we are all guilty of prejudice, and it would be unrealisitic to pretend that my own views might not colour my interpretation of certain events in this book.

There are, of course, many excellent books covering the development of the firms which operated and built Britain's buses, but there has been no book which traces the detailed development of the motor bus as a vehicle, from its horse bus origins right through to the expensive and sophisticated machines of today. Hence *The British Motor Bus*.

My aim has been to present an illustrated record of the reasons behind the many mechanical and design changes which have taken place over the 80-year history of the motor bus, related to the social upheavals of these eight decades and the competition the bus has faced from many sides. Because this book concentrates on the bus as a vehicle, detailed information on the growth of the operating industry, and the attendant mergers, take-overs and groupings, is omitted, although, of course, the main details are recorded where they relate to events on the vehicle side.

In his book *The Horse Bus as a Vehicle*, Charles E Lee dates the use of the word 'bus' as an accepted abbreviation of 'omnibus' to 1832 — adding, characteristically "regardless of the fact that, etymologically, it is a meaningless suffix of a Latin word, indicating only the dative plural". Nonetheless, in this book I have used the word 'bus' as a collective term to cover all types of motor buses and coaches.

I have restricted the book to buses in Britain. Where I have no personal memories of a particular era, I have endeavoured to include quotations from contemporary writings to convey some of the mood of the time and the changing attitudes towards passenger transport.

The story of the motor bus almost fits neatly into decades, but events have really decided the way the chapters are split. It is widely recognised that 1905 was the year the motor bus really emerged as a serious form of transport, so the first chapter traces the background of horse and steam traction up to this date. The end of World War I is another obvious turning-point in the story of the bus, and the major reorganisation of the industry in 1929/30 really relates to the decade that followed. World War II must be considered on its own, and the uncertainties of the early postwar years merit a separate chapter. Forty years after the upheavals of the 1920s came the 1968 Transport Act and its consequences, and 1969 is taken as the starting-date to bring the story up to date.

The story of the bus can never really be up to date, of course. It is an ongoing story that constantly fascinates those of us who are interested in buses, whether as staff, as students or — most important — as passengers.

Gavin Booth
Edinburgh.

What is This That Roareth Thus ?

We take motor buses so much for granted that it is difficult to visualise a time when London only had 17 motor buses in service, or when the Great Western Railway — of all organisations — was the biggest motor bus operator in Britain with 36 buses. Yet this was the case little more than 70 years ago.

Since these days the story of the motor bus has been a fascinating and varied one. It has faced competition from all sides; from electric tramcars, underground railways, motor cars, trolleybuses — even television. And it has seen the most wasteful type of competition in the often exciting bus-versus-bus, dog-eat-dog rivalries of the 1920s.

The bus has survived these assaults, though it would not be true to say 'unscathed'. Its role has, however, changed dramatically to suit changing economic and social patterns. Its original role was as a feeder to tram and underground services, but as the motor bus become more reliable, the motor bus turned the tables and gradually Leyland's 1920s slogan 'bury your tram with a Titan' became the order of the day.

After World War II and a brief return to the standards and popularity of 1939, the twin threat of television and widespread private motoring forced the motor bus industry to look in the mirror and reconsider its own image. And then, suddenly, the energy problems of the 1970s proved what the bus industry had been saying for years — that here was an economical and effective method of moving people.

For their part, the manufacturers, in their motor bus designs, have tried to reflect the changing needs of operators; on many occasions the manufacturers have led the way. 'What is this that roareth thus?' asked A D Godley in his well-known poem 'Can it be a Motor Bus?'. Often it was in those early days. In today's ecologically-minded world, the motor bus certainly shouldn't roar; the surviving handful of manufacturers who supply Britain's bus needs work within strictly-enforced noise limits — one indication, perhaps, of the increasing legislation affecting the bus today. This legislation reflects the place of the bus in the 1970s and it is not all restrictive. Bus priorities in cities, rural bus subsidies and bus grants towards new vehicles are just some of the positive steps which have emerged from a wider realisation of the potential of the bus.

All of which is far removed from the noisy and unreliable motor bus experiments of the early 1900s. To discover how these experiments came about, we must first look at the background of horse, steam and electric traction which went before. This, as they say, is where the story really begins.

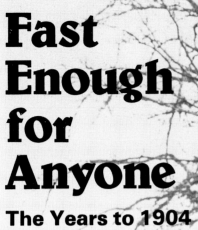

Fast Enough for Anyone

The Years to 1904

The pioneering nature of many early bus routes is captured by this early photograph of a Great Western Railway Milnes-Daimler on a rail feeder service.

Man has always wanted to travel. Some more adventurous spirits, in previous centuries, have tried to travel faster or farther than anyone else. But the common man was always content to live, work and play within a tightly-bounded environment — often because he had to. To him, transport was a horse or, more often than not, his feet.

The countryman living by the soil often lived and died without straying far from his birthplace. Even in the 17th century only the privileged few had personal transport, horse-drawn carriages, to move them in relative comfort. Most towns were still small enough to render public transport unnecessary, except, again, for the moneyed classes, who supported the hackney carriages or used their own sedan chairs.

Paris and London were the exceptions and for many years they set the example that other towns followed. In 1662, Blaise Pascal set up a service of *carrosses a cinq sols*, horse-drawn vehicles on regular services, but it was a venture which lasted only until 1675. A century later the French and English capitals had grown sufficiently to prompt men to consider new forms of regular public transport. The first mail coach, carrying both mail and passengers, was introduced between Bristol and London in 1784 and though this was an expensive way to travel, within 50 years there were regular mail coach services all over Britain. This new mobility appealed to the citizens of Britain's fast-growing cities and short-stage carriages were soon to be found on the streets.

Once more the French led the way. In 1819 Jacques Lafitte introduced 18-passenger short-stage coaches on a number of cross-city routes. Four years later Stanislas Baudry, of Nantes, started running coaches between his public baths and the centre of the city. The central stance was outside a grocer's shop, belonging to a M. Omnes, and gave the service the name *Omnes Omnibus*. The success of Baudry's service, not only with his bathers, prompted him to seek powers to operate a number of coaches on service in Paris. These were granted and in 1828 his omnibuses started on regular service in the Paris streets with a success that did not go unnoticed. Soon there were competitors for the business that Baudry had generated, and one by-product of this rivalry was the emergence of the man generally credited with the introduction of the omnibus to Britain, George Shillibeer. As a young coach builder in Paris, Shillibeer realised the potential traffic to be explored in his native Britain. He sold up and returned to London, where he built two 22-seat three-horse buses for a regular service between the Bank and Paddington Green or Marylebone

Road. This service commenced in July 1829 at a fare of 1s (5p) all the way with an intermediate 6d (2½p) fare to Islington.

The fares, which were cheaper than those charged on stage coaches, soon attracted what Shillibeer described as the 'middling class of trades-people' as a convenient compromise between the hackney carriage and walking. As in Paris, there were soon imitators. While Shillibeer had the foresight, his business sense was possibly not so keenly developed. He was bankrupt by 1835, and turned his transport talents to the business of funeral undertaking.

The others thrived and the horse-drawn omnibus went from strength to strength. For several decades the horse omnibus dominated urban passenger transport, but its elder brother, the stage coach, was threatened by a noisy newcomer.

Simple railways, wooden or metal tracks to guide wagon wheels and ease load-carrying, were common in industrial areas. Steam, the power behind the industrial revolution of the 19th century, was soon harnessed for stationary engines, and then for locomotives. The early, crude locomotives were regarded primarily as an alternative to horse-power for industrial purposes, but George Stephenson and some of his contemporaries realised their wider potential. Stephenson's Stockton & Darlington Railway is widely regarded as the first passenger-carrying steam railway, yet the Liverpool & Manchester, opened five years later, in 1830, was really the dawn of the new era — the first railway built primarily for passengers.

The 1830s and 1840s were decades of tremendous activity, as far-seeing speculators constructed railways all over Britain. The birth of the railways heralded an end to the golden age of coaching. As the railways built up, they bought over stage coach firms to link up with their trains. Stage coaches lingered on for many years in those areas not blessed with the new-fangled railways, but horse-drawn transport in its other roles was far from dead. Passenger transport in towns was to remain firmly horse-drawn until the 1880s, in spite of numerous attempts to change all that. There had been experiments with steam road vehicles, but these were never very successful. High tolls, bad roads and fierce legislation were the main factors against steam coaches, but men like Richard Trevithick, Sir Charles Dance, Walter Hancock and Scott Russell were undeterred by these problems and some of their vehicles were even used in service. Increasing resentment and suspicion, coupled with the appalling state of many roads, combined to dampen the enthusiasm of their inventors. Oddly enough, the steam railways played their part in killing steam coaches; with the disappearance of long-distance stage-coaches, as the railways spread throughout Britain, the country roads fell into disrepair.

For Shillibeer, read omnibus

Back in the towns, horse buses were developing fast. In London there was great rivalry between operators and competing coaches often raced each other for passengers. There were other abuses, too. Many of the buses were poorly built and badly ventilated; some operators overcharged; others misused the Shillibeer name. But 'Shillibeers' did not catch on, and 'omnibus' became the accepted term. The existence of 'Shillibeer's Funeral Carriages' may have hastened this change!

The omnibus was a simple vehicle, a box-like structure with two rows of inward-facing longitudinal seats, for 12 passengers in all. Entry was through an outward-opening door in the rear wall. A critic described the interior of the early horse bus as 'nothing but a couple of narrow shelves on which passengers are packed like trussed fowls on the ledge of a poulterer's window'. As traffic grew, the operators looked for ways of packing more passengers into their buses. The extra bulk and weight, combined with the narrow streets, prevented bigger vehicles, so passengers had to be carried on top. The first double-deckers of the 1840s had a longitudinal seat on the open upper deck, but by the Great Exhibition of 1851, held in London's Hyde Park, the 'knifeboard' bus had appeared. This featured a central back-to-back bench seat for an extra ten persons.

The Great Exhibition was a much-needed shot in the arm for the horse bus. The extra traffic which was attracted into London spawned a whole host of new services and new operators. Among them was one man whose name was to become increasingly familiar over the years; Thomas Tilling, who started 'The Times' horse bus service from Peckham to the West End. Right from the start Tilling insisted on civility, and realised the importance of regular timetabled services. The Tilling family went on to operate motor buses, building up an impressive empire which was eventually nationalised, ultimately to form an important part of today's National Bus Company. But we are jumping ahead.

In the 1850s Londoners at least were becoming transport-minded. *The Illustrated London News* in April 1856 reported:

'As a large majority of the citizens of London undoubtedly prefer the vehicular to

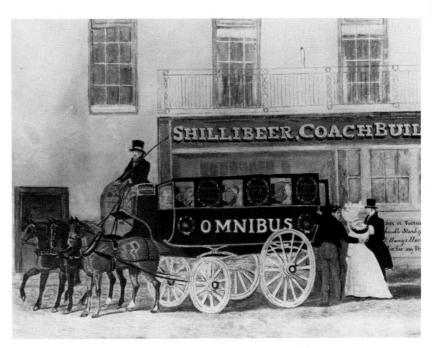

the pedestrian mode of locomotion, they may be fairly supposed to entertain some curiosity repecting the details of a system which undertakes their migratory propensities to the very utmost.

'We are so much accustomed in this most practical of all possible countries to sing the praises of commercial competition, that it requires some moral courage to demand public applause in favour of an avowed monopoly.

'And yet, as the exception is said to prove the rule, it should not be subject of special wonder that circumstances may combine to justify an occasional doubt as to the correctness of the national theory.'

The 'avowed monopoly' was the Compagnie Générale des Omnibus de Londres.

Once more the French led the way. The Paris horse bus system had been reorganised in 1854, and a similar exercise was proposed for London. The new *compagnie* was registered in Paris, and through British agents it set about amalgamating the existing London bus operators. The new association was welcomed by the public and the press. After the Great Exhibition, the reduced traffic provoked fresh competition and the poor state of some of the buses, combined with the congestion which even then was clogging London's streets to disillusion and confuse the travelling public. Hence the 'public applause' for the Paris enterprise, which had started to take over existing businesses in 1855, ready to start operations in January 1856. There were only 27 General buses at this time, but by the end of 1856 there were over 600 in service. Not all of London's horse bus proprietors sold out to

Passengers are ushered aboard one of George Shillibeer's Omnibuses, which first started operating in London in 1829. They attracted what Shillibeer described as the 'middling class of trades-people'.

Twenty years after Shillibeer, and the horse bus was already changing in shape and layout. This horse-bus, with knifeboard seating on the upper deck, linked two suburbs of Edinburgh in the 1850s.

the new company; some, like Tilling and Birch, held out, and remained familiar names in the transport world over a century later.

The General company went from strength to strength, and became the basis for the giant that is now London Transport. In 1859 the business had been transferred from Paris and became the more familiar London General Omnibus Company.

But while London General gradually improved travelling conditions in the Metropolis, there was horse bus activity in most of the other large centres of population in Britain. By the 1860s, enterprising businessmen had followed the London example and had set up horse bus services with varying degrees of success. In Glasgow, the appropriately tartan-clad horse buses of Andrew Menzies were described by one observer as 'dreadfully uncomfortable. Passengers on the top deck were exposed to the weather. Inside, there was no ventilation and on wet days the floor was covered by damp, smelly straw.'

There were efforts to improve these conditions, however. London General ran a competition, with a £100 first prize, for 'the best design of omnibus that, with the same weight as at present, will afford increased space accommodation and comfort to the public'. A Mr Miller of Hammersmith, a coachbuilder, won the prize, but his design was not adopted; instead, London General pinched the best ideas from all the entries. They also examined buses acquired from Edinburgh, Glasgow, Birmingham and Wales in their efforts to gain more passenger space and improve conditions.

Something to be avoided
The 'teething troubles' experienced in

London are described in the centenary history *London General*:

'At the beginning of the period, in the early 1860s, the fortunes and indeed the reputation of the company had been at a very low ebb. Matters were not made any easier by the strings of hansom cabs which, loitering for chance fares, daily impeded traffic in the city. The appalling state of the roads, together with the fierce struggle necessary to secure a place on a bus, the "absurdly inefficient" space allotted to each passenger once aboard, poor ventilation, the "general pushing and hustling, insinuating and retorting", made bus travel (according to the *Illustrated Times* of the day) something to be avoided "except under pressing necessity". "In what year of the present century", asked this journal, "shall we behold all these improvements which were to be the immediate result of a conveyance monopoly?"'

Harsh words. But things did improve, and by 1874, one journal could enthuse in these terms:

'The efficiency of the service of the London General Omnibus Company is proverbial, while the attention at all times given to the complaints of passengers as well as to the interests of the Company, by its active Secretary, Mr Augustus George Church, is admitted at once, and while every route in London is so admirably served, indeed, that it is next to an impossibility not to travel from anywhere to everywhere either in London or its suburbs, without comfort and rapidity'.

It was just as well that the General had supporters like this, for in 1881 a new operator took to the London streets. The London Road Car Company gained its strength in the same way as the General, by buying over smaller operators, and it was soon a source of many problems to its rivals. The 'road car' name had been chosen because 'omnibus' had foreign connections — as, of course, had London General. The patriotism of the new firm was emphasised further by the fleetname Union Jack and the small flag carried at the front. A contemporary broadsheet entitled 'No Surrender' welcomed the newcomers as 'Pioneers of all improvements, handsome cars and cheaper fares'.

Road Car was no cheeky upstart, as General was soon to discover. One of the new company's first improvements was the introduction of a new design of horse bus. Passengers boarded by a proper platform and access to the top deck was by a proper staircase. At first the platform and staircase were mounted at the front, behind the driver, but it soon reverted to the rear, setting a basic pattern that was to remain virtually unaltered on double-deck buses for over 80 years. There was one other important improvement. The upper deck seating was on two-seater transversely-mounted seats, the garden seat rather than the 'knifeboard'.

The arrival of Road Car did much to improve the standard of the horse bus as a vehicle and of the service itself. For the last few decades of their existence, horse buses enjoyed an Indian Summer. So much so, that in 1898 *The Bus, Tram & Cab Trades Gazette* could write:

'Everyone rides in omnibuses in these democratic days. The character of these useful public vehicles has entirely changed during the past few years, and the old lumbering fusty-smelling coach with its manifold drawbacks has given place to a clean, roomy conveyance in which the comfort of the passenger is studied in every way.'

The success of the railways and of horse buses led men to consider some form of street railway. Needless to say, Paris led the way in 1855 and five years later a young American, George Francis Train, came to Britain to sell the idea to anyone who would listen to him. These street railways were the first tramways, and the first successful lines in Britain were laid in Birkenhead in 1860. Horse tramways spread through Britain over the next 20 years, often with horse buses providing connections. The initial cost of the permanent way was considered prohibitive in some centres, but by 1880 most towns of any size had tramway networks.

There were other rumblings at this time — quite literally in some cases. Legislation had killed the steam coach, but the steam tram encountered fewer obstacles, and in the last 30 years of the 19th century a number of tramway systems employed steam power quite successfully, normally using steam locomotives which towed separate passenger trailers. Other systems, fewer in number, adopted cable traction where the trams gripped a continually-moving cable under the road. This was fine as long as the cable was continually moving, powered by steam-driven pulleys. When the cable broke — and it frequently did — parts of the system simply slowed to a halt. Britain's best-known cable trams were in Edinburgh, where they lasted until 1923. In the United States, the famous San Francisco cable cars still operate to this day.

It took two other Victorian discoveries to

change all that — in fact they changed the face of the world. First came electricity and, more particularly, electricity as a motive power. And just as the world was learning how to use electricity, along came the internal combustion engine.

For a change it was the efforts of the Germans, and not the French, that assisted in the birth of the electric tramway — or rather the efforts of one particular German, Dr Werner von Siemens, whose name is also associated with early trolleybuses. Using a converted horse tram with an underfloor motor, Siemens opened a 1½ mile electric street tramway near Berlin in 1881. In Britain, only two years later, Magnus Volk opened an electric tramway on Brighton beach — a tramway that still operates during the summer season. In spite of Volk's

Top: **A peaceful Victorian scene in Cheltenham's High Street, after the introduction of the electric tram, but before the arrival of the motor car.** *Above:* **The final version of the London General horse bus, with transversely-mounted garden seats on the top deck. This basic body style was fitted to many early motor buses, and even the body on the famous London B type had its origins here.**

13

All eyes on the camera, outside the Eyre Arms, St. Johns Wood; a London General knifeboard-type horse bus about 1890.

pioneering efforts and other early efforts in Northern Ireland and Blackpool, Britain rather lagged behind in its acceptance of electric tramways. The problems of current collection may have contributed to this reticence, for the early tramways relied on third rails, mounted between the running rails — or even at the side; in the case of Blackpool the conduit system was used, with a cable-style slot between the rails, beneath which was the conductor rail.

There was fresh interest in electric tramways when, towards the end of the 1880s, a successful system of overhead wires and spring-mounted trolleys was developed. Britain's first overhead tramway was opened at Leeds in 1891 and this opened the floodgates. The electric tram became a matter of fervent municipal pride and most towns were eager to augment and replace their horse trams with the new-fangled electric trams, which proved to be quicker and cheaper than any previous method of urban transport. They were also smoother, at a time when many roads left much to be desired; and they were big and undeniably impressive, beautifully constructed by craftsmen, and painted in elaborate liveries that echoed the civic pride. The electric trams encouraged white-collar workers to live further from their places of work and contributed much to the outward sprawl of many British towns and cities.

The electric tramcar enjoyed its heyday in the Victorian and Edwardian eras, before any of the alternate means of transport had really developed. The first electric system closed down as early as 1917, the start of a constant process which continued until the 1950s and 1960s, when the last of the real

British street tramways gave way to the motor bus. The tramcar is still very much with us, of course. It never achieved the success in Britain that it has enjoyed in recent years on the continent, with complex and impressive rapid transit systems far removed from the traditional British concept of the tram. Tyne & Wear PTE is presently developing a light electric railway that will, in effect, be a rapid transit tramway, and Blackpool and the Isle of Man — amongst the electric pioneers — still retain their highly individual systems. The 'enemy' (if we are to believe the pro-tram/anti-bus faction) was the internal combustion engine, and we must return to our story, again to Germany, to find how this developed.

Two names are irreversibly linked with the earliest successful experiments to produce motor vehicles powered by petroleum spirit. Karl Benz and Gottlieb Daimler were both working independently to harness the petrol engine to drive a road vehicle, and in 1885 they each unveiled the results of their endeavours. At one of Benz's earliest public demonstrations, an observer recorded:

'Without any sign of motive power, such as that generated by steam, and without the aid of any human element, such as is necessary with a velocipede, the vehicle rolled onwards, taking bends in its stride and avoiding all oncoming traffic and pedestrians. It was followed by a crowd of running and breathless youngsters. Those who witnessed this strange spectacle could scarcely believe their eyes. The suprise was as general as it was great.'

The motor car had arrived, and the

Continentals were quick to recognise its potential. German and French names crop up most frequently in the annals of early motoring and the first successful British enterprise is remembered, appropriately enough, by the pioneering German name of Daimler.

A young and inventive British engineer, Frederick Simms, met Gottlieb Daimler in 1890. Simms was impressed by Daimler's experiments and negotiated an agreement by which Simms acquired all Daimler engine patent rights for Britain. In 1893 Simms formed a small private company to handle Daimler products, the Daimler Motor Syndicate Ltd. The syndicate was taken over in 1896 and the Daimler Motor Company Ltd was formed, using a former cotton mill in Coventry to produce private motor vehicles, the first built in any quantity in Britain. Daimler was shortly to enter the bus market too, but that belongs to the next chapter.

An important year
The year 1896 was an important one for the motor vehicle in Britain. First there was the Highways Act. It was a serious attempt to update outmoded legislation like the Locomotives Act 1865 (the infamous Red Flag Act, which restricted 'road locomotives' to 4mph in the country and 2mph in towns, behind a man carrying a red flag). The 1896 Act removed the most stringent of the early regulations and eventually a speed limit of 12mph was fixed.

Another event of 1896 which was to have a far-reaching effect on the British motor industry, both in the private and commercial fields, was the founding of the Lancashire Steam Motor Company. This small firm built

steam vehicles, including some buses, and might well have disappeared into the mists of time but for the energetic direction of Henry Spurrier and James Sumner. Many important orders were secured and in 1897 Spurrier told Sumner: 'If we don't make this firm a success now, we deserve to be kicked. We've got the world by the pants and a downhill pull.' The firm was a success, and in 1907 it became Leyland Motors Ltd, notable as probably the first of the pioneering manufacturers to concentrate purely on commercials, and the foundation of today's giant British Leyland empire.

Steam and battery-electric buses enjoyed a brief spell of popularity in the last years of the 19th century, following the Highways Act. Some years before, as if in anticipation, a battery electric bus was operated experimentally in London. In 1889 Radcliffe Ward obtained a Metropolitan Police licence for his battery bus, described by the *Financial Times* as resembling 'a large and rather cumbrous omnibus.'

The bus was never used in service, but Radcliffe Ward was not discouraged. He introduced a 10-seat single-deck battery bus in 1897 which was intended for service in London, but it, too, never ran in public service. Two years later the Motor Omnibus Syndicate Ltd was equally unsuccessful; this syndicate obtained a licence for a 24-seat double-deck Gillett steam bus, but it was never to run in regular service.

It was 1899 before a petrol-engined bus could be seen in service on London's streets, but the rest of the country was quicker off the mark — the strict control exercised by the Metropolitan Police had a strong influence on the development of the London bus for many years. Outside London, the wagonette was often the first mechanised public service vehicle seen on the streets. The wagonette was rather like a large private car, with an open rear section containing inward-facing benches. The Edinburgh Autocar Company introduced what is regarded as the first *licensed* urban service in May 1898, using Daimler and MMC wagonettes, although the venture failed in 1901. The licensing system was very vague at this time; there had been earlier motor bus experiments in various parts of Scotland and England in 1897, though these had not been licensed. The wagonette enjoyed a brief success, though by 1906 it was being replaced by vehicles which were more bus-like and less car-like.

Back in London there was a new threat to the established bus and tram services — the underground railway. The first underground railway, the steam-worked Metropolitan, had opened in 1863, but the real threat came in the 1890s and 1900s. The first electric tube railway was the City and South London, opened in 1890, and this was followed by the Waterloo-Bank line in 1898. These early lines had a noticeable effect on the buses operating on parallel routes, creaming off the longer-distance traffic and leaving the buses to provide a feeder service. With the opening of the Central London line in 1900 — the 'twopenny tube' — the horse bus proprietors realised that something had to be done to combat this new competition. But what?

London's population had doubled in the period 1851-1891 and by 1901 had reached a staggering 6,500,000. This combination of factors prompted many of the experiments with mechanical buses. One of the most

important was the operation of two Canstatt Daimlers (built in Germany) with 26-seat former horse bus bodies between Kennington and Victoria, from October 1899 to December 1900. Therefore, as Charles E Lee observes in *The Early Motor Bus*, 'the twentieth century opened without a single motor bus regularly plying in the Metropolis.'

During the early years of the new century there were many experiments with mechanised road vehicles in all parts of Britain. The records are incomplete, as there was no formal vehicle licensing on a national basis. In London the Metropolitan Police kept a close eye on all such developments and elsewhere it was left to the diligence of the local Watch Committee. Often there was literally no licensing at all. For this reason we know more about activities in the Metropolis than about the developments in the rest of the country.

We do know about two events of 1903 which were to create important precedents. Eastbourne Corporation had rejected the idea of a tramway system and sought and obtained Parliamentary powers to operate buses within the borough; on 12 April it started motor bus services with four Milnes-Daimler 16hp single-deckers. This first municipal enterprise was not without its critics, for only four months later a protest meeting was held in the town 'condemning buses and calling for a proper system of electric trams'.

Further west, between Helston and the Lizard, in Cornwall, the Great Western Railway started a bus service. This first ran on 17 August and again used Milnes-Daimlers, 16hp 22-seat wagonette-type vehicles. These petrol buses had originally been bought to run in conjunction with the Lynton & Barnstaple Railway, but there was such strong local opposition that they were soon sold to the GWR. The Helston-Lizard service was the GWR's answer to demands for a light railway: the bus service was to test the market, without incurring too much expense, whereas the estimated cost of the railway was £85,000. This was not the first railway bus service; there had been steam buses operated by the Belfast & Northern Counties Railway in 1902 and, of course, the Lynton & Barnstaple's short-lived experiment, but the GWR service is particularly important as the first step towards the largest of all the railway bus fleets.

The petrol-engined motor vehicle was still very much a novelty at this time, a plaything for the rich, not to be taken too seriously. The traditionalists grumbled that 'a carriage and pair is fast enough for anyone —

A group of adventurous souls leaving Helston for the Lizard in 1903, aboard a Milnes-Daimler in the GWR fleet. The service was started to answer demands for a light railway, and although it was not the first railway bus service, it was the first step in the creation of GWR's large railway bus network.

comfortable, safe, and smart; moreover, it is certain to reach its desired destination.' The Continental manufacturers still led the way, with France and Germany in the lead; it is interesting to note that it was not until 1906 that car production in the United States exceeded that of France.

In Greater London in 1901, 848 million passenger journeys were made. Buses carried 270 million, trams 341 million and local railways carried the rest. In London in 1901 these trams were still mainly horse trams, for the Metropolis was surprisingly slow to adopt the electric tram which was by then a common sight throughout Britain. The London United Tramways service from Hammersmith to Shepherds Bush, which started in 1901, was London's first proper electric service, but the electric tram was never really allowed to develop in London as it had done in many other centres in the country.

The design and development of the early motor bus was largely hampered by unrealistic legislation. The Government tended to assume that all buses were either mechanised horse buses — admittedly some of them were — or large motor cars like the wagonettes already mentioned. Pressures from bus proprietors and manufacturers prompted the Motor Car Act of 1903, which raised the speed limit for 3ton vehicles to 20mph, and also introduced vehicle registrations with effect from 1 January, 1904. Further legislation, the Heavy Motor Car Order of 1904, raised the unladen weight to 5tons at a top speed of 12mph.

All of this activity at Westminister played a decisive part in the real birth of the bus and 1905 is widely regarded as the birth date. In 1904, however, the seeds were laid.

Throughout the country, enterprising men were setting up companies to operate buses. Many of these ventures were destined to be short-lived, but others laid the foundations of firms that are with us today. In the south-east of England, for instance, two companies were formed during 1904 which were later to merge as part of the Southdown undertaking. The Sussex Motor Road Car Company actually started operations that same year, initially with two Clarkson steam buses. The Clarksons were unsuccessful and were soon sold and replaced by Milnes-Daimlers, but the company was successful. According to *The Southdown Story*, 'there was an enterprising, even, one might say, a faintly swashbuckling air about its doings that is not unattractive.' This was just as well, for a rival company, the Worthing Motor Omnibus Company, was formed towards the end of 1904. Inevitably there was soon competition, particularly for the Worthing-Brighton

service, and the more firmly-based Worthing company survived the Sussex company, which went into liquidation within a few years.

There were many reasons for the early demise of so many motor bus companies. The drivers and mechanics were dealing with unfamiliar machinery, and the buses themselves were still very crude and prone to breakdown.

An important landmark

The event of 1904 which was to change much of this was the introduction of the Milnes-Daimler 24hp 34-seat double-decker at the Crystal Palace Motor Car Show in February. Daimler patents had been used for many of the earliest petrol engines, and in 1902 the old-established tramcar builders G F Milnes & Co Ltd entered an agreement with the German Daimler company to build Daimlers under licence in Britain. Originally, 16hp single-deckers were built, and these could be fitted with either enclosed single-

The introduction of the Milnes-Daimler double-decker in 1904 was an important landmark in the story of the motor bus. It set a pattern that was to be widely imitated, and this advertisement appeared in the trade press early in 1905.

Top: A 25hp Brush Mutel 23-seat covered charabanc delivered to the Potteries tramway company in 1905. Like many of its contemporaries, the chassis could be found carrying a charabanc or a double-deck body, or even, as in the case of this vehicle, an overhead tower wagon. *Above:* London General's very first petrol-engined bus combined a normal horse bus body with a Swiss-built Orion chassis. It started running between Hammersmith and Piccadilly in December 1904.

deck saloon or enlarged wagonette bodies. But the 1904 double-deck model represented an important landmark in the story of the British bus, the first really practicable, purpose-built bus, setting a pattern that was largely unchanged until 1919. The driver sat behind the engine, in the open, but under a canopy which kept him reasonably dry, if nothing else. The enclosed lower deck had inward-facing seats for 16, with access from the rear platform. The outside staircase led to the 18-seat open upper deck, which had forward-facing seats. The high-built wooden body still had many traces of its horse-bus origins, but it was to be many years before bodybuilders broke away from this concept.

The Milnes-Daimler double-decker was an instant success, and many of the pioneer motor bus fleets started operations with small fleets of these buses. Two of London's pioneers in 1904 were certainly not new to bus operation. On 30 September Thomas Tilling Ltd, a successful horse bus operator since 1851, placed three Milnes-Daimlers in

service in London; on 11 October another two Milnes-Daimlers started running in London, for Birch Bros. Ltd. The Birch family were also horse bus owners, but their motor bus venture was less successful than Tilling's. J M Birch later recalled that 'the roads were very bad, the machines very unreliable, the drivers very inexperienced and the maintenance staff ignorant.' The Birch family pulled out of the motor bus business after only three years and by 1912 had given up their horse buses as well. They were to return, though, as bus and coach proprietors.

And where were London General and London Road Car while Tilling and Birch were introducing regular motor bus services to London's streets? To be honest, they were rather slower to appreciate the potential, although at the same time as the Tilling and Birch Milnes-Daimlers started to run, both General and Road Car were experimenting with single-deck steam buses. These were 14-seat Chelmsfords, built by Thomas Clarkson, whose name will crop up again in this story, and Road Car had two and General one. Urban single-deck buses enjoyed a brief spell of popularity at this time, but relaxed regulations allowed double-beckers to flourish.

Between 1899 and 1904 a total of 92 motor buses had been licensed by the Metropolitan Police in London, 79 single-deckers and 13 double-deckers. And even as 1904 drew to a close, there were only 17 motor buses in service in London. Five of these were the Tilling and Birch Milnes-Daimlers already mentioned; London Power Omnibus Company had 9 Scott-Stirling single-deckers; London Road Car had 1 Germaine and 1 Dürkopp; and London General had 1 Orion 26-seat double-decker. This was General's very first petrol-engined bus, a horse-bus body on Swiss-built Orion chassis. In spite of General's lack of success with its mechanical experiments, it was beginning to realise where the future lay. The company chairman admitted that General had 'studied the causes of their failure' and had 'observed various difficulties gradually surmounted'. He went on: 'We feel the time has now come when services of motor omnibuses can be successfully run by us'. To support this new-found confidence, General set aside £20,000 for experiments with motor buses. London Road Car, too, started to move in the same direction, with a large order for motor buses. Even so, they were still a long way behind the Great Western Railway, whose 36-strong motor bus fleet was, ironically enough, the largest in the country in 1904.

But big things were about to happen in 1905 — and that was just the start.

When London General coined the phrase 'Open Air to Everywhere', no one anticipated the Great War and London buses on troop-carrying duties in France and Belgium. These MET Daimler Y types are seen in Flanders Village.

Open Air to Everywhere

1905–1918

In the first years of the 20th century the motor bus had taken its first faltering steps towards its serious acceptance as a means of public transport. The first part of the story seems strongly London-biased, because that is the way it was; London's requirements for public transport were inevitably the greatest in Britain, but the growing industrial towns and cities were setting their own patterns. The railways still carried the majority of longer-distance travellers, with, in country districts, horse or motor buses providing connections from stations to outlying villages. In most towns the electric tram was the predominant mode of transport, and again the bus provided feeder services, often linking tram termini with new housing developments or with less accessible spots where the cost of new permanent way would have been prohibitive.

This short-distance role was not adopted voluntarily. The motor bus was still far from reliable, and rural roads did not encourage comfortable long-distance travel. Town roads, though better, were well served by the electric trams, still a fairly recent addition to the urban scene, and one that represented heavy civic investment. In any case, the fast and comfortable tram compared favourably with the simple, often unreliable, solid-tyred motor bus.

To be honest, the population was still not motor-minded. Even London General, by far the biggest horse bus operators in Britain, remained vocally pro-horse until about 1910.

The motor bus therefore had to prove itself, and establish its role in the overall transport pattern. Some regarded the bus as second-line transport, complementary to trams or underground trains; others — with more vision, foresaw the days when the flexibility of the motor bus would threaten the future of the tramways — perhaps even the railways. By 1905 some of these men were already active, and although the structure of the bus industry does not really come within the scope of this book, it is useful to look at nine brief case histories to illustrate a trend that was gradually emerging.

Case Histories

The financial backers who founded the Scottish Motor Traction Company in June 1905 could have had no idea that their optimistically-baptised brainchild would, in fact, literally live up to its name, for within 25 years SMT became parent company of the SMT Group, basis of today's Scottish Bus Group. One man can take much of the credit for the success of the venture, William

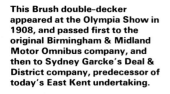

This Brush double-decker appeared at the Olympia Show in 1908, and passed first to the original Birmingham & Midland Motor Omnibus company, and then to Sydney Garcke's Deal & District company, predecessor of today's East Kent undertaking.

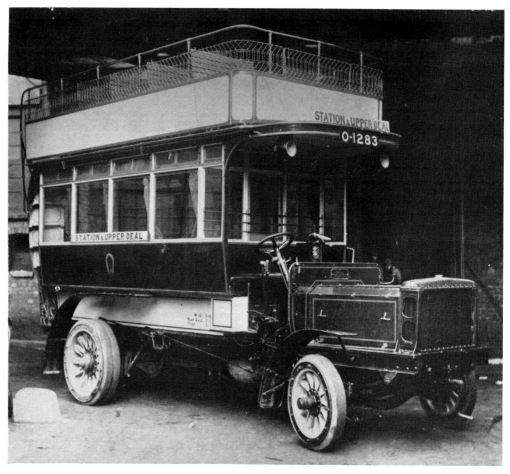

J Thomson, a Caithness man who became the SMT's first engineer. He drew up a stringent set of requirements which he expected his buses to reach. Several different types of motor bus ordered for trial purposes failed to meet his stringent conditions, that a top speed of 12mph should be achieved and that the bus should be able to reach 3mph on a 1 in 3 gradient, fully loaded. Only one make fulfilled his conditions, a 40hp double-deck Maudslay, and nine 35-seat double-deckers were ordered to start SMT's first public services, on 1 January, 1906. The local press failed to appreciate the importance of this event, as little mention was made in their pages; possibly they pre-judged SMT as yet another over-ambitious upstart. This was not the case, of course, and SMT went from strength to strength, initially with Maudslays and Ryknields, and eventually with an advanced home-made vehicle which will be described later in this chapter.

Just south of the Scottish border, another small bus operator was becoming established, taking the first steps towards a widespread empire and carrying a name that is still very familiar today. E B Hutchinson's United Automobile Services had actually been formed to take over some Great Eastern Railway routes in East Anglia in 1912, but the next year another branch of the business started operations in County Durham, in the Spennymoor-Bishop Auckland area. Like most of the early motor bus operators, United's development was steady, but slow, until the end of World War I. Then in the mushrooming 'bus mania' of the 1920s, United expanded at both ends until it eventually covered a vast area of England, from the Scottish border down to East Anglia. The area was later split, leaving United to operate mainly in Northumberland, County Durham and Yorkshire, where the familiar red buses can still be found today.

The British Electric Traction Group was an active product of the 1890s, its purpose being the carriage of passengers and goods, and the generation and distribution of electricity. Ironically, it was not only an electric tramway pioneer, but also a motor bus pioneer, and its buses were to supersede the trams, laying the foundations for a huge company bus empire which was only absorbed in 1968 by the Tilling Group. The Barnsley & District Electric Traction Company was formed by BET in 1902 to operate tramways in and around Barnsley. Only eleven years later the company started a bus service in an area where tramway extension was impossible, using five Brush-bodied Leyland single-deckers costing £822

each. The buses flourished, and the trams floundered, to the extent that the word 'Electric' disappeared from the company name in 1919; a more radical name change in 1928 reflected the expansion which the buses had permitted — the Barnsley-based fleet became the Yorkshire Traction Company.

Another BET venture was the Potteries Electric Traction Company, operating in North Staffordshire. The first PET trams ran in 1899 and only two years later the company was experimenting unsuccessfully with steam buses. In 1905 three Brush-Mutel 25hp double-deckers were bought to provide feeder services for the main tramway routes, but these too were unsuccessful. PET's next bus venture was more significant, when four Daimler single-deckers appeared in 1914; although the buses were impressed for military service in World War I, they returned to form the basis of a large fleet. The PET trams were finally withdrawn in 1928, killed not only by the company's own buses, but by the unrestricted competition of the 1920s which brought a total of 81 bus operators into Stoke on Trent at one stage. The company's old name lasted until 1933 when the familiar and more appropriate title Potteries Motor Traction — PMT — was adopted.

In the thriving city of Birmingham there were several early attempts to promote motor bus services. The Birmingham Motor Express Company started operations in 1903 with three single-deck Napier-engined Mulliners. The company required additional

Halifax Corporation bought three Daimler CC models in 1912; this one, with an enclosed rear-entrance bus body, is seen negotiating some of the town's notorious hills.

Early deliveries to two pioneering fleets. Top: **The Scottish Motor Traction company started operating on January 1, 1906, and by 1913 had developed its own home-made bus, the Lothian. This was a notable advance in layout, for the driver sat alongside the engine, rather than behind it, allowing more passenger space.** *Above:* **The Bristol Tramways & Carriage company started operating just 11 days after SMT, and this was one of its first vehicles, an Italian-built Fiat 24/40hp chassis, with a Dodson 36-seat body, bought for £850. In this case the driver sat over the engine, reputedly to help manoeuvrability in crowded streets.**

capital the following year, and the new Birmingham & Midland Motor Omnibus Company was incorporated to take over the Express company; in 1905 various BET bus interests, motor and horse, were transferred to the new company. The original BMMO company was, rather surprisingly, unsuccessful, and motor buses were abandoned in 1907 — in favour of horse buses! With better buses, the BMMO motor buses bounced back in 1912 and went from strength to strength. Midland Red, as the company is universally known, became the largest company bus fleet in Britain.

Birmingham also had one of the early municipal bus fleets. The Corporation introduced ten double-deck Daimler Y types on tramway extension routes in 1913 and in 1914 entered an area agreement with BMMO which included the transfer to

Birmingham Corporation of 30 BMMO Tilling-Stevens double-deckers.

The coming of the motor bus to Oxford was quite a different matter. In 1881 the City of Oxford & District Tramway Company started running with four horse trams, and inevitably electrification of the system was soon being actively discussed. The main difference at Oxford was that electric trams never did run in the streets. While various interested bodies were busy talking, Mr W R Morris announced that he was to introduce a motor bus service in December 1913. This he did with two Daimler Y type double-deckers which ran in competition with the horse trams; inevitably, the trams suffered. Morris's Oxford Motor Omnibus Company bought more Daimlers, and operated them equally successfully — so successfully, in fact, that the tramway company offered to run buses instead of the proposed electric trams. Thomas Tilling also wanted to run buses in Oxford, and the three rivals submitted vehicles for inspection late in 1913. Licences were granted to Morris and to the tramway company, but when the tramway buses appeared Morris withdrew to avoid wasteful competition. The Morris name was not destined to disappear; soon he was involved in the lucrative business of building the cars which carried his name, for this was the same William Morris who later became Lord Nuffield, whose factories generated much business for the company which in 1930 had adopted the more familiar name City of Oxford Motor Services.

Bristol, always a busy and go-ahead city, was fortunate in having the Bristol Tramways & Carriage Company as its local operator. The company's horse tram system had been electrified in the last years of the 19th century, and in 1905 it was testing a Thornycroft bus. The outcome of this trial was the first regular bus service, which started on 17 January, 1906. Not only did Bristol Tramways quickly appreciate the potential of the motor bus, but the company also built its own chassis, starting in 1908. The motor side of the business grew rapidly; by 1914 there were over 60 miles of bus routes, served by 44 buses and 29 charabancs. Today, both Bristol Omnibus (the operating company) and Bristol Commercial Vehicles (the manufacturers) are notable names in the British bus business.

When BMMO withdrew from motor bus operation in 1908, Sidney Garcke bought six Brush double-deckers and brought them to Deal in Kent. Using three of the buses, with the other three as spares, Garcke started regular services in April 1908. There had been earlier motor bus experiments in East Kent, but Garcke's Deal & District Motor

Services was the most successful, and soon there were other operators chasing the passengers. The shortages and other problems of World War I prompted Garcke to engineer a merger between these companies, and in 1916 the East Kent Road Car Company was formed to take over the five main competitors. The new fleet inherited 72 buses, a mixture which included Albions, Commers, Daimlers, Leylands, Straker-Squires and Tilling-Stevens.

Catching up

After the Continental domination of the early years, it is interesting to note that most of the new maker's names appearing in the case histories were of British origin. Home manufacturers were at last starting to catch up, and between 1905 and 1919 foreign-built buses virtually disappeared; similarly, the British manufacturers who relied on Continental patents evolved designs of their own. The needs of the London motor bus operators and the strict legislation imposed by the Metropolitan Police tended to dictate the fashion for the rest of Britain. London was clearly the biggest potential motor bus market, and ambitious manufacturers were naturally anxious to carve themselves a slice.

Names like De Dion, Orion, Lacoste & Battman, Dürkopp and Germaine made way for the home-produced chassis. In spite of the plethora of new British motor bus builders, there was very little difference in the basic layout of their early products. Like the trend-setting Milnes-Daimler of 1904, the typical chassis was essentially straightforward and uncomplicated. The four-cylinder petrol engine was mounted at the extreme front, over the front axle. The size of the engines varied, usually between 20-40hp; to transmit the power from these strong. low-speed engines to the solid-tyred rear axles, most manufacturers fitted the differential unit to the chassis and drove each rear wheel by a side chain. The distinctive chain final drive of early motor buses worked well, if noisily, but gradually the worm-driven differential rear axle was developed and improved, becoming universally fitted.

The manufacturers of the day merely offered a commercial chassis for sale and the customer used it as he wished. Consequently the high-built straight chassis were equally at home with double-deck, single-deck or charabanc bodies and were also used for lorries. Some operators took advantage of this imposed versatility; double-deck and charabanc bodies were often swapped to cater for weekday commuters and weekend excursionists. In fact, many smaller operators fitted a lorry body during the week and a charabanc body at weekends. The only

people who did not benefit from the adaptability of early commercial chassis were the passengers, who had a stiff climb into those early buses and a rough ride once they were there. It was to be many years before these problems were overcome.

In the last chapter we looked at the Milnes-Daimler double-decker, which set a trend that remained largely unchallenged for 15 years. The equivalent single-decker was in most respects a double-decker without the upper deck and staircase, but the charabanc was quite different. A development of the horse-drawn charabanc, the motor charabanc enjoyed tremendous success in the early motor years. Very often it gave Britons their first experience of the motor vehicle and opened up a new market in leisure travel as the charabancs reached out to seaside or countryside which had

A section of the Leyland stand at the Olympia Show in 1913, with a 32-seat 'torpedo' charabanc for Armitage of Blackpool, mounted on an S type chassis.

A Daimler CC charabanc delivered to the Provincial Tramways company at Grimsby in the immediate prewar period.

previously been too far for comfortable day outings.

The driver and the passengers sat together in an open body on full-width seats which were usually reached by side doors, one door on each side to each seat. There was a hood folded at the back for the often-inclement weather, which provided cover at the top, but not at the sides. Some charabancs had permanent top covers with open sides, while some vehicles, not charabancs in the strictest sense, had a raised rear portion, essentially for better vision. The *Worthing Gazette* described the appearance of a Sussex Motor Road Car Thornycroft at Worthing in 1908 thus: 'The new type of vehicle is a sort of wedge-shaped pattern, the several successive rows of seats being placed tier above tier, so that the upper part of the charabanc is raised very considerably above the front section. It weighs about five tons in all and is licensed to carry thirty-two passengers.'

Not all of the new British commerical vehicle manufacturers were destined to achieve the success they sought and very few of the names of 1905 are still with us. Some, like Arrol-Johnston, Scott-Stirling and Straker-Squire, lasted for only a few years; others, like Albion, Dennis, Maudslay, Thornycroft and Wolseley, were to remain familiar names for very much longer — though not necessarily on buses. Inevitably, many operators favoured local products, and this ensured respectable sales figures. Other makes were more widespread, like the Milnes-Daimler already described.

The Milnes-Daimler and the Straker-Squire, another popular model in the late 1900s, were built in Britain, but Milnes-Daimler used German Daimler designs, while the Straker-Squire used German Büssing patents.

Original thoughts

Not all of the new British designs were entirely conventional, though. Among the pioneers were some innovators, and there were lessons to be learned from their original thoughts — although often as not their efforts convinced other manufacturers *not* to follow suit.

There was Thomas Clarkson, who had been trying hard to sell his steam buses for several years. Clarkson built the Chelmsford steam buses which London General and London Road Car used in 1904, and in 1905 Road Car received the first of a number of Clarkson double-deckers. The Clarkson steam bus was a neat and relatively successful design, but Clarkson, like so many of his contemporaries, relied on London orders. When London General decided to abandon steam in 1909, Clarkson created work for his buses by founding the National Steam Car Company, which built up a fleet of around 180 of these unusual vehicles. National changed over to petrol buses when the Clarksons came up for replacement, and Clarkson himself left the company to set up in business outside London, a decision which was to have an important effect on the later development of company buses.

Another unusual model of the time was Daimler KPL, an amazingly advanced double-deck model. Built by the Coventry Daimler firm, the type name was derived from the initials of Knight, Pieper and Lanchester, who designed the engines, transmission and worm drive respectively. The KPL introduced many advanced features. There was no separate chassis, for the underframe and body were constructed as one all-steel unit; there were brakes on all four wheels; it had petrol-electric transmission; and the two 12hp engines were

A selection of Sheffield Corporation's first buses, all 40hp Daimler CCs delivered in 1913.

mounted beneath the main structure, each driving a rear wheel. Tilling raised a patent infringement action which effectively killed off both the KPL and Daimler's attempts for form a bus company in London to operate them.

The Tilling objection covered the petrol-electric transmission, for the Tilling management had been interested in the possibilities of petrol-electrics for some time. The consequent lack of gears and a clutch made it easier for horse bus drivers to adapt to motors. Tilling-Stevens was a joint venture between Thomas Tilling and W A Stevens of Maidstone, and the company's first TTA1 double-decker entered service in 1911. The Tilling fleet was the main TTA1 operator, but they were sold commercially, and Tilling-Stevens achieved reasonable success with successive petrol-electric models over the years. In 1924 Tilling sold its manufacturing interests, but Tilling-Stevens continued to build buses for many years, though after the mid-1920s these were to conventional designs more often than not.

Another operator with an interest in developing a reliable bus suited to its needs was SMT, based in Edinburgh. William Thomson, as engineer of the company, was looking for something better than the Maudslays and Ryknields which had helped to put SMT on its feet, and started on his new design in 1910. It was a long process but Thomson knew what he wanted, and, as one of his colleagues recalled later, 'he was a difficult man to argue with.' SMT's first home-made bus, the appropriately-named Lothian, emerged in 1913. It was 23ft long, and had a straight frame chassis fitted with a four-cylinder 38hp Minerva Silent Knight sleeve-valve engine. There was a four-speed chain-driven rear axle. Solid tyres were fitted.

The 32 seats were divided into two 'compartments', for non-smokers and smokers, and the cutaway rear entrance set a Scottish trend that was followed for many years. Three large sliding windows were fitted — predecessors of today's panoramic windows in many ways.

Most novel of the Lothian's many features was the driving position, which was alongside, rather than behind, the engine. This allowed a high seating capacity within the dimensional regulations of the time, and pioneered a layout which rapidly became accepted as standard throughout the country.

The Lothian, then, was very much ahead of its time. It was faster, smoother and quieter than the existing SMT buses, and as production got under way, allowed the older bus fleet to be replaced. The first Lothians were 32-seat saloons, but in 1915 a 31-seat charabanc version was introduced.

Around 90 Lothians were built for SMT between 1913 and 1924, and some even received pneumatic tyres. The Lothians soldiered on in regular service until around 1927, when they were relegated to lighter and duplicate journeys. Even so, a number lasted until 1930, a considerable tribute to their construction in an era of short-lived buses.

Steady growth in London

After its slow start, the motor bus really established itself in London during the decade after 1905. From the 17 motor buses licensed in London at the end of 1904, the numer grew steadily. There were 241 by the end of 1905, 1,000 by 1908, and 2,000 by 1913, and not all were owned by General, Road Car or the other former horse bus proprietors like Tilling or Birch. In March

LONDON GENERAL OMNIBUS
COMPANY LTD

MAP and GUIDE
TO
OMNIBUS SERVICES

PEARS'SOAP

GENERAL

OPEN AIR
TO
EVERYWHERE

NOVEMBER 1912
ISSUED MONTHLY

A drawing of the famous London
General B type bus featured on
the company's map (*above*) in the
pre-Great War period. The real
thing (*facing page*) is seen in this
1914 London street scene.

1905 a completely new motor bus operator appeared, the London Motor Omnibus Company, trading under the fleetname Vanguard, which was displayed prominently on the sides, starting a new trend.

Vanguard started with five Milnes-Daimlers, and stole a march on its competitors by obtaining a priority on deliveries from the Milnes-Daimler works. The well-run Vanguard fleet soon represented a serious threat to the longer-established names, who were faced with the problems of replacing their horse buses, converting existing garage premises and re-training staff. The continental manufacturers were quick to cash in on this situation though with varying success. The De Dion chassis was popular with London General, and dominated the fleet for a few years.

As the fleets grew, so did the rivalry — and inevitably this became wasteful. Things seemed to happen too fast. In 1907 *Tramway & Railway World* said: 'The motor bus business in London was rushed. It came before its time. The mechanism of such a vehicle had not been duly perfected, and the pioneers have now to pay the penalties.' After a bad year in 1907, when a fatal combination of low fares and bad weather brought extra problems to London's bus operators, General, Road Car and Vanguard got together to find a satisfactory solution. The outcome was a merger in 1908, and a new, big London General company. The new combine owned 885 of the 1,066 buses in service in London at the time, dominated by 356 Straker-Squires, 312 Milnes-Daimlers, 165 De Dion and 75 Wolseleys.

Frank Searle was the new combine's chief motor engineer, and faced with such a mixed collection of buses he set about designing an efficient vehicle for fleet replacement. His design was seriously affected by new Metropolitan Police regulations, issued in 1909, which laid down very stringent guidelines for operators in London. Buses had to be no more than 23ft long, 7ft 2in wide, with a maximum of 34 seats (18 up/16 down), and, worst of all, no more than 3½ tons unladen (6 tons laden). Such a low unladen weight was virtually unheard of, and at first it was feared that the regulations would stunt the growth of the motor bus. Undaunted, Searle worked on.

The new General company had inherited a useful factory at Walthamstow which had been used by Vanguard to build and repair vehicles, and here Searle built his first X type, a double-decker which satisfied the Poilice requirements. It went into service late in 1909, and Searle later wrote: 'In the manufacture of the X type we cribbed

shamelessly; any parts of the 28 types which had stood up to the gruelling of the London streets were embodied in it.' This caused some critics to describe it as the 'Daimler-Wolseley-Straker' type, but its success was to confound them. Experience with the X type led to Searle's second design for General, one which was certainly a further milestone in the story of the British bus, the famous B type, which first entered service in 1910.

Here was the first standard bus, a purpose-built reliable and efficient vehicle which did a lot to put the General company back on its feet, and sounded the final death-knell for the horse bus. Around 2,900 B types were built, mostly double-deckers, and most had a 30hp 4-cylinder engine, a 3-speed gearbox and a worm-driven rear axle.

The B type gave London General the firm foundation it required. The motor bus network grew rapidly, and early General bus maps proclaimed proudly 'Open Air to Everywhere' as the bus swept onwards and outwards.

The manufacturers react
The other manufacturers suddenly found themselves with two big problems. There was the effect of the Metropolitan Police regulations, which was gradually overcome by new, lighter designs; then there was the virtual disappearance of their biggest potential source of business. There was not such an easy answer to this one. Leyland, eager for a foothold in London, invested in the London & Suburban Company, which became London Central, and eventually New Central, with a sizeable fleet of Leyland double-deckers. Thomas Clarkson, as already described, had similar ideas, and so did Daimler, with their proposed Premier fleet of advanced KPL buses. Daimler wanted Frank Searle to be general manager of Premier, but when General and Tilling conspired to bring the patent suit against Daimler, the operating plans were dropped and instead Searle was lured away to start Daimler's commercial vehicle department. Not surprisingly, a new Daimler 40hp double-decker, bearing a strong resemblance to the B type, appeared in 1912, and after a **certain amount** of wheeling and dealing Searle won an order for 350 buses from the BET Group. These were mainly for a BET subsidiary in London, the Tramways (MET) Omnibus Company; this new operator was formed by Metropolitan Electric Tramways to run in association with the MET trams, mainly as a safeguard against the prospect of increased competition from London General.

While all this was happening, General was undergoing yet another change in ownership.

The Underground Electric Railways Group saw the expanding and improving General as a threat to its underground railways, started buying up General shares and assumed control early in 1912. Under its new masters, General bought up some of its competitors and entered into agreements with others. Tramways (MET) was acquired in 1913 and Daimler found that General did not wish to continue the maintenance contract which was part of Searle's deal with BET; instead, Daimler was appointed as sole selling agent for any surplus chassis produced at Walthamstow.

General's bus-building activities at Walthamstow had also been affected by the change of control. The Underground Group felt that sales of Walthamstow products to outside operators were hampered by the connections with General. So the connections were severed and a new Underground subsidiary, the Associated Equipment Company, was formed. Under its more familiar intitials, AEC, the new firm soon started to sell to a wider public.

The charabanc and the trackless

As the motor bus became more reliable, it became more widely accepted throughout Britain. Its main function was still short-distance urban transport, but there were far-sighted operators exploring longer-distance

bus services, and there was the growing charabanc business already mentioned. A development of this which reflected the increasing reliability of the bus was the introduction of extended tours. Surprising as it may seem, Chapman's of Eastbourne offered a six-day North Wales tour as early as 1910, using a Dennis 22-seater. The success of this venture prompted Chapman's to expand the programme and soon passengers were setting off on a 21-day tour to John o'Groats! Other companies followed this lead, like Standerwick of Blackpool and Worthing Motor Services. The Worthing firm adopted the title Sussex Tourist Coaches, and ran its first extended tour, to the west country, in June 1913. A passenger wrote of the large crowd which greeted the tour at Exeter, apparently attracted 'by the novelty of our car'. Clearly, the motor bus was still far from universally accepted, and even then there was a new competitor on the scene.

The trackless car, or trackless trolley, was the forerunner of the trolleybus, which was to enjoy the peak of its success in the 1930s. Werner von Siemens can take much of the credit for the invention of the trackless car, but it took commercial enterprises to bring these new hybrids to Britain. Railless Electric Traction was one of the main firms attempting to interest British operators in

This 1913 centre-entrance Commer WP of Commercial Car Hirers later became one of the first vehicles operated by Trent Motor Traction. Note the high build of the vehicle, and the passengers sitting alongside the driving position. The 23-seat body was built by Scammell.

trackless cars, and these attempts included practical demonstrations, as at Hendon, London for MET in 1909, and visits to inspect systems on the continent. Dundee, Leeds and Bradford Corporations all sent deputations to Europe in 1908/9 and all showed a keen interest in this new type of urban transport. Leeds and Bradford were sufficiently interested to apply, successfully, for powers to run trackless vehicles. The first parts of the two systems started within days of each other in 1911; Leeds probably won the race to operate Britain's first trolleybus in service, but Bradford had the more questionable honour of operating Britain's last, over 60 years later.

The trolleybus does not strictly belong in this book, except as a rival for the motor bus, but it is interesting to recall just how some of the early systems fared. Most of Britain's trolleybus pioneers were in the northern part of England where, as well as Leeds and Bradford, there were Rotherham, Keighley, Ramsbottom, Stockport, Teesside, and Mexborough & Swinton; but there were also outposts in Wales, at Aberdare and Rhondda, and in Scotland, at Dundee. The Dundee system was particularly interesting; as early as 1908 a deputation of Corporation officials visited Germany to inspect trackless systems and were suitably impressed. 'The trackless trolley system of traction', they concluded, 'is undoubtedly practicable and well suited for routes where the traffic would not warrant the construction of an ordinary tramway, and the sub-committee are satisfied that there is more likelihood of success with this system than any other'. In this same enthusiastic mood, Dundee Corporation opened its trolleybus system in 1912 — and closed it in 1914. The short life of the Dundee system was attributed more to the Corporation's reluctance to spend enough money on road improvement than to any doubts about its efficiency or its financial performance.

With the demise in Dundee, there remained only eight trolleybus systems in Britain when World War I broke out in 1914. The war inevitably affected public transport throughout Britain. There was little material damage to bus, tram or trolleybus systems, but there was a growing shortage of suitable staff, which led to interrupted services and played havoc with regular maintenance. Bus operators suffered from vehicle shortages, as the War Office commandeered suitable motor buses for military service. Only the petrol-electric buses were really safe, since the War Office chose not to requisition them. London General's large motor bus fleet was a popular source of vehicles for war service; General

temporarily lost more than 1,500 buses, mostly B-types, and many of these were sent to the battlefields of Belgium and France.

The shortage of petrol brought extra problems to the operators who were still able to maintain bus services — often essential services to military and naval establishments. Many bus companies overcame the fuel problem by running on coal gas, carried in cumbersome gas balloons fixed to the bus roofs. These gas buses were crude, but guaranteed a service which could not otherwise have been provided.

World War I brought the development of the motor bus grinding to an abrupt stop. By 1918 the buses that were returning from war service were often in poor condition, for at the time the average lifespan of a bus was only five or six years. The setback was only temporary, though; the war had proved the versatility of the motor vehicle and the next decade was to see a dramatic and exciting renaissance.

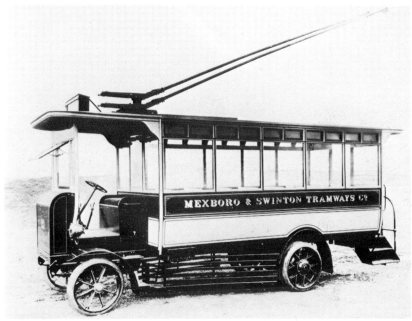

Top: **Haslingden Corporation's first bus was this 1907 Leyland X type with 18-seat Leyland body. Its basic construction was, of necessity, sturdy and straightforward.** *Above:* **An early trackless trolley, a Brush-bodied Daimler of 1915. It was the first such vehicle supplied to the Mexborough & Swinton Tramways company.**

Cut and Thrust

1919-1928

Many people might remember the 1920s as a period of unrelieved economic gloom. True, there was severe and prolonged unemployment — during the decade there were never less than 1 million unemployed in Britain. For others, though, living standards rose with the increase in owner-occupied housing and the growth of new council estates.

The bus certainly blossomed in the ten years following World War I, but it was not a controlled development — indeed at times the cut-throat competition suggested that the fledgling motor bus industry had a death-wish. Competition was certainly the keynote of the period and this competition had several effects. It forced all sections of the bus industry to take stock and resulted in vastly improved vehicles, sensibly-integrated groups of companies and proper all-embracing legislation. Tramways and railways suffered as the motor bus grew in stature, while the bus itself faced new problems from the increasing popularity of the private car. In transport, at least, the Twenties were certainly Roaring.

The war played its part in convincing many people that the motor vehicle had a rosy future. The success of the mechanical involvement in the war proved this to the faceless men in authority, while actual experience with motor vehicles persuaded many newly-demobilised men to invest their gratuities in transport as a business. And there were many men eager to help former Tommies to realise this ambition, by selling them chassis.

Initially, these were often vehicles reconditioned after war service, medium-size and simple chassis like the RAF-type Leyland, Daimler Y and Thornycroft J. The new chassis offered by the British builders were little different in 1919. The established bus operators had lost many of their buses during the war and were anxious to re-stock; for convenience they took chassis types that were basically 1914 designs. The keen newcomers to the bus industry were at first forced to follow suit, but when a veritable flood of foreign chassis was released on to the British market, they had less chauvinistic qualms than their established brothers.

This new invasion force started its attack on Britain in the early 1920s, plugging a glaring gap in the domestically-produced ranges. They came from France, Italy and the United States, and they were cheap, small and fast — on pneumatic tyres. Pneumatics for commercial vehicles were still being developed at this time and could only be used satisfactorily on lighter commercials. Most of the imported chassis were in the 14-26-seat range and were designed as passenger vehicles; they were not the dual-purpose goods/passenger types normally available in Britain.

The instant success of these imports introduced many new names to Britain's roads and the best-remembered names sold in reasonable numbers, like the Chevrolets, GMCs and Reos from the United States, and the Fiats and Lancias from Italy.

Armed with these fast and attractive little buses, bus operators sprang up all over the country. Some pioneered new routes, while other elbowed their way on to existing services. A quick profit was the common denominator throughout, and often there was nothing in the way of a formal timetable — buses ran as and when prospective passengers appeared. There were sometimes literally dozens of one-bus operators on some of the best routes.

The outcome of such unrestrained rivalry was inevitable. Some busmen fell by the wayside; some went on to consolidate their position by acquiring their less organised contemporaries; others banded together to strengthen their position and a few of the 'safety in numbers' co-operatives of the 1920s survive to this day. The operators who lacked business acumen often more than made up for this with a brand of low cunning. Buses literally raced each other for passengers; buses turned short to pick up customers; and buses happily switched routes if the driver thought there were better pickings elsewhere. But it would be wrong to suggest that these attitudes were universal. Some operators were well organised, with proper timetables and schedules, efficient staff and a proper regard to the provision of a public service. These, it is interesting to

Facing page: **Competition for the charabanc traffic at the Mound, Edinburgh, in the early 1920s. The vehicles shown include Leylands, and Thornycrofts, and two Scottish-built vehicles — a Halley (nearest camera) and a Clyde (centre).** *Below:* **One of many ex-RAF Leylands brought back and refurbished after the Great War. This one received a Leyland rear-entrance body.**

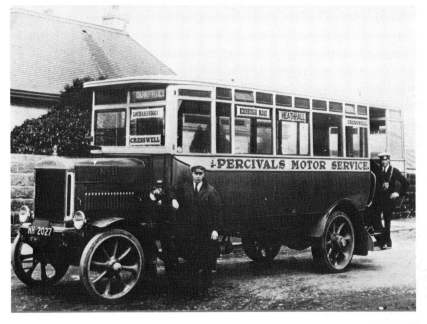

add, were the firms which usually survived, and which are still in business today.

A wide choice

The arrival of the foreign chassis added considerably to the number of different makes which British operators could buy. By 1926 there were more than 55 makes of bus chassis on the British market; just over half of these were of British origin, with 12 from the United States, seven from France, two from Italy, two from Switzerland and one from Belgium. Not all of these firms were successful. Far from it. Many were unable to survive in this highly competitive field, while other decided to concentrate on truck chassis. The sales of foreign buses gradually tailed off towards the end of the 1920s as British builders started to catch up. After the slow recovery from the war, the success of the light foreign buses spurred the main manufacturers into action. A look at some of the more popular models illustrates the advances.

This was essentially an era of single-deck development, for the use of the double-decker was still relatively restricted outside London. The most important new models were, therefore, single-deckers and the Leyland Lion is probably the best-remembered product of the time. Leyland's five-model L range appeared in 1925 — the Leopard, Lion, Lioness, Leveret and Leviathan. All were conceived as passenger models, and consequently lower-built and more refined than the previous goods-cum-passenger chassis. Of the five new models only the Lion was a real success in sales performance. More than 2,500 Lions were sold in four years, and this put Leyland back on its feet after a difficult period immediately after the war.

The Leyland Lion LSC1 — subsequently the PLSC1 — was a forward control model, with the driver sitting alongside rather than behind the 5.1litre four-cylinder petrol engine. It had a plate clutch and four-speed sliding-mesh gearbox. Leyland-built bodies were fitted to a good many of the Lions produced, for Leyland had a thriving bodybuilding department for many years.

In the 1920s it was common practice for operators to get local builders to body their bus chassis; the days of the really big national bodybuilders, supplying to the whole country, were still to come. British bus operators have always indulged in the strange practice of buying chassis at one end of the country, which are then bodied in another part of the country and possibly then delivered to a third, quite different, part of the country. Only a few of Britain's chassis builders have tried to provide a complete service and Leyland has been most successful. Leyland's functional wooden-framed body style for its Lion chassis was a much imitated classic of its time.

The rash of imported chassis had brought a wider acceptance of forward entrances, immediately behind the front wheels. Other than charabancs, most single-deckers previously had rear entrances, often on platforms, double-deck style. Now forward

Right: **The French Berliet was just one of the many small, refined and fast buses imported in the early 1920s, although the Berliet name was not to become as familiar in Britain as Fiat, Lancia and Reo.** *Below:* **A 1925 scene in Perth with a Lancia from the Hepburn fleet, and its proud crew.**

entrances were in vogue, although the rear entrance had its advocates, as did the centre entrance — and there were operators who tried to improve passenger flow with two doors, front and rear.

The Leyland Lion is the best remembered lower-built model of its generation, but it was not the first. In 1924 Maudslay introduced its ML range, a comprehensive selection of models of different sizes and layouts; the Maudslay 4.94litre four-cylinder petrol engine was most commonly fitted to this steady-selling range. As the other manufacturers caught up, a rash of new models hit the market, and the most significant were the full-size forward control single-deckers with four-cylinder petrol engines, and suitable for 25ft-long 32-seat bodies — chassis like the Tilling-Stevens Express, the Bristol B, and Dennis E and the Albion PM28.

Some manufacturers chose to explore new fields, and the later part of the 1920s is often remembered as the heyday of the rigid six-wheel motor bus. Guy and Karrier were two of the early advocates of six-wheelers. Goods models were soon followed by passenger models, first from Karrier in 1925 and then from Guy in 1926. Karrier's 1925 prototype was a normal control single-decker; an improved version, the WL6, went into production in 1926 and about 160 single and double-deckers were built until the model was withdrawn in 1930.

Many advantages were claimed for the six-wheeler, including greater safety, better riding comfort and improved fuel and tyre economy. Certainly the early six-wheelers hastened the acceptance of pneumatic tyres on heavy passenger vehicles, and the use of single rear wheels increased internal body space. The six-wheel bus was a convenient way around the current Ministry of Transport regulations governing the maximum weight on each individual axle. By spreading the load, longer buses were possible; some were up to about 30ft, roughly 5ft longer than the average four-wheel bus of the time. This allowed higher seating capacities, 40 on a single-decker and 66-72 on a double-decker, and in larger towns and cities this extra capacity was very useful.

Guy's first six-wheeler created quite a stir when it was first revealed in 1926; not only was it the firm's first six-wheeler, it was also a double-decker — again Guy's first! The Guy BX was a normal control model, with a 5.1litre engine, and was followed by the forward control FBKX in 1927. Sales of this truly massive-looking bus were quite healthy and improved models stayed in production until 1933. The Guy was involved in intense

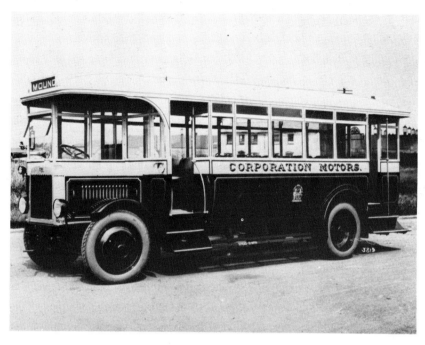

A classic of the 1920s, a Leyland Lion PLSC1 with Leyland bodywork, one of eight two-door 29-seaters supplied to Edinburgh Corporation in 1926.

rivalry between manufacturers shortly after its introduction in 1926, to see which make would first appear on service. Guy won the race in the provinces, at home-town Wolverhampton in July 1926, but another Guy was beaten to the post in London by a London General ADC in June 1927.

The life of the six-wheel motor bus in the provinces was largely confined to the 1920s and 1930s. Some operators continued to buy the double-deck chassis that were available right until 1939, and the six-wheel single-decker was to enjoy brief spells of popularity in the 1930s and, more surprisingly, in the 1960s. London was the main protagonist of the six-wheeler, though its interest can be traced from the end of the 1920s, first on a large fleet of motor buses and then on its huge trolleybus fleet. These will be examined more closely in a later chapter, but it is appropriate at this point to take a look at London in the 1920s: to go back, in fact, to 1919 to see the war-ravaged and reduced London General fleet struggling to maintain its services.

London's postwar problems
In the early days of the motor bus, London's requirements had set the fashion for the rest of the country, but in the 1920s the absurdly strict limitations imposed by the Metropolitan Police, coupled with General's apparent inability to move with the times, meant that the design of the London bus was generally out of step with developments in the rest of the country.

London General entered the post-World War I era with a smaller operational fleet that it had in 1914. Many of the buses requisitioned for military service never

An impressive machine by any standards — a massive-looking SMC (Sunbeam) Sikh six-wheeler of 1929, fitted with a 29ft long Dodson 67-seat body.

London's first postwar standard double decker, the K type, seen in later days in Metropolitan livery.

returned, while others were in poor shape. As a temporary measure around 100 lorries were fitted out as simple buses and these lorry buses helped to reduce some of the problems caused by the postwar demands on public transport. A new standard design of London double-decker was quickly produced and the first of 1,132 K type buses appeared in 1919.

The K type was a joint development by AEC and General, both, of course, members of the Underground Group. The AEC chassis had a 28hp four-cylinder engine, a multiplate clutch and a chain gearbox. The open-top General body was flush-sided, with wheel arches, permitting extra interior space. For the first time General was able to fit transverse seats on the lower deck, thus increasing the seating capacity to 46 (24/22), 12 more than on the B type. The open rear platform and staircase were similar to the B type's, though wider, but the main advance was the adoption of a forward control layout. As *Motor Transport* reported at the time:

'Increased accommodation for passengers is gained through saving the space that the driver at present occupies between the bonnet and the body of the vehicle. The bonnet is built up to the front of the omnibus itself, and the driver sits on the right-hand side in a recess cut in the bonnet and protected by a shield. He sits higher up, and as the exhaust gases escape on the left-hand side, he is much cooler than on the older

type'.

The K type was certainly an advance on previous London buses, though the poor driver, in his exposed position at the front, might not have agreed so readily. Outside London, drivers had been happily and safely enclosed in cabs or behind glass windscreens for at least ten years; it was to be another ten years before buses in service in London would be permitted this 'luxury'. A longer version of the K, the 35hp S type, followed in 1920, with seats for 54 passengers; in all, 928 S types were built.

On 4 August 1922 London General had a virtual monopoly of bus services in the Metropolis. The following day an independently-owned brown-painted Leyland double-decker appeared on the famous route 11. It started a reaction that was to have far-reaching effects on London General and on the design of the motor bus. The full story of the London independents — the pirates, as they became popularly known— does not really belong here, but some background notes will give some idea of the scale of the competition confronting the General.

The Chocolate Express Leyland prompted a slow trickle of other independent operators to venture on to the lucrative General routes. In just over a year this trickle had become a steady stream and by 1925 there were over 600 independent buses on London's streets. Inevitably, the independents concentrated their efforts on the money-spinning routes, competing not only with General but also

Karrier waxed eloquent about its
six-wheelers in this 1927 advert,
but users were often less than
lavish in their praise for these
unhappy models.

among themselves for traffic. Their methods
were not always entirely ethical and on many
occasions this competition verged on open
warfare, with buses literally racing each
other for custom. It would be wrong to
suggest that all the independents adopted
these tactics, for there were many responsible
and dedicated men among the new London
busmen.

These were not only exciting years, they
were colourful too, for distinctive liveries and
fleetnames were worn by the independents.
In addition, their buses were different. The
products of General's associate AEC were
obviously unavailable, so Leylands,
Dennises, Straker-Squires and Thornycrofts
flooded the streets. There was of course no
route licensing at the time and the operators
had only to satisfy the Metropolitan Police
that their vehicles were roadworthy within
London restrictions. The manufacturers,
eager to break into the London market, built
special buses designed to suit the London
regulations.

Leyland's fast and reliable normal control
LB chassis was popular with the early
independents in London, as was the Dennis,
again a normal control vehicle. Two forward
control chassis which could be found in
many independent fleets in London were the
Straker-Squire and the Thornycroft J. The
Straker-Squire was not the most reliable
vehicle of its time, as Clem Preece recalls in
his book *Wheels to the West*. Early in his
long and varied transport career Preece went

into partnership as an independent bus
operator and he remembers the A type
Straker-Squire as 'mechanically very
advanced for its time. The vehicle certainly
had a high power/weight ratio and, despite
solid tyres, was quite fast; unfortunately, it
tended to shake itself to pieces as a result.
For the cut and thrust of pirate bus work, the
quick acceleration and speed were a great
advantage, if only the vehicle could have
been more reliable.'

Just as the independents could not buy
AECs, General's connections with AEC —
and probably its innate pride — prevented it
from shopping around for more and faster
chassis to allow more even competition.
General was, however, developing a better
double-deck model which was a definite
advance on the horse bus concepts of the B,
K and S, and which proved a transition
between these early designs and the
sophisticated new models of the late 1920s.

The new model, the NS (standing,
apparently, for *Nulli Secundus* — second to
none) was designed from the outset as a low-
built, pneumatic-tyred, covered-top bus and
no doubt General saw it as the answer to
their pirate problems. Unfortunately the
Metropolitan Police did not see it quite the
same way and the first NSs of 1923 were
open-topped, on solid tyres. Like the K and S
before it, the NS was a forward control
model, but the poor driver was still exposed
to the elements. About 2,400 NS models
were bought by General between 1923 and

1930, and AEC sold NS-based chassis on the open market as the 409 and 422 models. The last General NS buses were able to appear as the design was originally conceived. They had pneumatic tyres, first introduced in 1928, and top covers from 1925. The driver did not have a windscreen, but special NS vehicles for working through the Blackwall Tunnel did have fully enclosed staircases.

Pneumatic tyres were first seen outside London on lightweight single-deckers in the early 1920s, they were eventually developed to suit heavier single-deckers from around 1923 and six-wheel double-deckers from 1926. The Metropolitan Police resolutely held out until 1925 and in that year pneumatics were permitted on General's single-deck K types; two years later they were fitted to General's six-wheel LS double-deckers, but they were not allowed on the NS until 1928.

Covered tops had been successfully fitted to double-deckers long before the birth of the NS. Widnes Corporation had four covered-top Commers in 1909, and Liverpool and Birmingham led the way in the 1920s. But the Metropolitan Police insisted that 'no canopy or similar superstructure will be permitted on the roof of an omnibus constructed to carry passengers on the top deck'. They stuck firmly to this view until public opinion and reports of satisfactory operation outside London persuaded them to permit top covers from 1925. A press report of the time described the top-covered NS thus: 'Passengers find them much more comfortable than the old type of bus which is being replaced. There is room for 28 passengers in the padded top-deck seats,

One of the London 'pirates', Alfred Temple Bennett's London Public company, introduced 14 of these Guy FBKX six-wheelers on the London streets in 1927.

handrails up the gangways, sliding plate-glass windows, rubber padded — a real luxury vehicle. They do not appear unwieldy and the public are enjoying the experiment of riding in a covered bus, and during a rainy spell, instead of there being a scramble for the inside seats, the competition is to get to the top and look at the unfortunate people on the old buses shrinking under waterproof sheets'.

While London top deck passengers fared better from 1925, London bus drivers were exposed to all weathers until 1929, when glass windscreens were allowed at last — at least 20 years after operators throughout the rest of Britain.

In spite of all these problems, the NS was an important step forward. Its low build made life easier for passengers and it helped London General to fend off the competition from the independents. A correspondent in *Commercial Motor* in 1925 suggested that General 'would not have been stimulated to build the admittedly excellent NS type but for the new competitors'. There is probably more than a grain of truth in this, but with General, bus replacement was a major exercise. Any new London design has a long gestation period and ideally should be adaptable enough for a long production run. The NS certainly fulfilled this requirement, for the basic design was sound enough to permit the later additions, pneumatic tyres, top covers and driver's windscreens.

The last NSs were, strictly, built by ADC, rather than AEC. In 1926 AEC combined with Daimler's commercial vehicle business to form The Associated Daimler Company, selling vehicles built by both concerns. Both AEC and Daimler designed chassis were built, normally offered with a choice of AEC or Daimler engines. The alliance was fairly short-lived and in 1928 the two firms returned to their separate ways; in fact they remained quite separate until coming together, more forcibly, under the British Leyland umbrella in 1968.

One purpose of the ADC set-up was to allow AEC to complete the transfer of production from the old Vanguard works at Walthamstow to a new factory at Southall, and when AECs — complete with the familiar triangle badge — started to appear from Southall they were, inevitably, simply developments of ADC designs. AEC's most exciting bus chassis of the 1920s really belong in the next chapter and so, too, do the far-reaching developments which led to the restoration of General's monopoly. But in the mid-1920s General was still battling with the so-called pirates and the situation was rapidly getting out of hand. The official reaction was the 1924 London Traffic Act,

which restricted the number of buses permitted to operate on certain streets and obliged operators to submit schedules for approval. Operators could not always get permission to run on the routes they chose and they were required to provide all-day services. Deprived of the quick-change, traffic-chasing tactics of the early independent days, many of the smaller operators fell by the wayside. Some simply disappeared, while others merged and others sold out to General. Although a few independents held out for five or six more years, by 1928 the pirate threat had all but disappeared

Competitors all round

So much for competition within the bus industry; what of the competition from other sources? Just as the 1920s witnessed a dramatic leap forward by the motor bus, the decade was equally important for the motor car.

Between 1919 and 1924 the number of private cars on Britain's roads quadrupled; between 1924 and 1930 this total doubled again and by 1930 there were over a million cars in Britain. These figures were boosted by models like the Austin 7 of 1922 (selling at £165) and the 1928 Morris Minor (£125). Motorcycles, too, enjoyed a boom in the 1920s, their peak year was 1930, when 724,000 were licensed.

The railways, on the other hand, did not enjoy much prosperity in the decade after World War I. Run down after the war, the railway companies reorganised in 1923 and no sooner had the four new main line companies emerged under the Grouping than they began to realise that the bus was a serious competitor. From 1925 there was a long and bitter fight between the bus and railway operators as they both sought wider official powers. The railways were actively campaigning for powers to operate bus services; there were still the railway bus services, but the main line companies were thinking on a much grander scale.

The success of the motor bus was also having its effects on tramways. Although there were 14,000 trams in Britain in 1924 — the all-time maximum — the tram was already in decline. During the 1920s 34 smaller electric tramways systems were replaced by motor buses and in the same period another 11 systems were replaced by trolleybuses, for the trackless tram was still in the ascendant. True, some of the earliest systems had already closed down, but there were some important converts in the 1920s, among them future strongholds like Wolverhampton, Ipswich, Darlington, Doncaster and Maidstone.

Charabancs to coaches

Leisure travel by bus continued to spread in the 1920s, firstly in charabancs, and with the introduction of more suitable, lower-built chassis from 1925, in fully-enclosed 'all-weather saloon coaches'.

A happy party of excursionists pose with their coach at Land's End in 1927. It was a BMMO QC 30-seater, one of five supplied in that year to the Trent fleet.

'The charabanc of the post-war period was a cumbersome monstrosity mounted high on a chassis which swayed dangerously on corners', wrote *Tramway and Railway World* in 1930, adding that 'Owing to its solid tyres and inadequate springing, [it] provided little in the way of comfort for its occupants'. The 29 intrepid passengers who set out in July 1920 in 'one of Mr Alexander's handsome and well-appointed motor charabancs' on an extended tour to John o'Groats might well have agreed with these sentiments, but *The Falkirk Herald* reported at the time that it had been 'a delightful tour' and that the grateful passengers had presented Mr and Mrs Alexander with a solid silver set of tea knives. Spurred on by this success, no doubt, Mr Alexander went on to start bus services in the Falkirk area and Alexanders became one of the main company operators in Scotland.

The new motor coaches prompted operators to consider longer-distance services, and 1925 really saw the birth of the express and long-distance network we know today. The actual date can be accurately pinpointed, for on 10 February 1925, Greyhound Motors of Bristol inaugurated an express service to London, the first daily long-distance express coach service in Britain — and probably in the world. Two solid-tyred Dennises started the service, but pneumatic-tyred AECs were soon added. In 1927 four 'super de luxe buffet coaches' were added to the Greyhound fleet, ADC 416As with Strachan and Brown bodies. A contemporary report describes these amazing vehicles, and emphasises the tremendous advance over the charabanc:

'The latest type of omnibuses put into service on this route are each divided into three main sections, the front and largest of them containing eighteen seats, arranged in the conventional manner, the centre having on one side a lavatory, and on the other a small buffet; while the rear part, which is the smoking saloon, contains seats for eight persons. All these seats are padded and covered with red antique leather, and are fitted with head rests. At the back of each seat, for use by the passenger in the seat behind, is a small oval mirror, together with a gusseted pocket for holding newspapers and such-like articles. By pulling a tab a small table is unfolded, which is arranged in a position convenient for holding a lunch tray. Beside each seat is a bell-push for summoning the steward; and a further convenience is found in the electric light switch controlling the roof light installed over each seat.

'Heat from the engine exhaust can be directed and used to provide warmth for the interior... At the back of the driver's compartment there are a clock, barometer, flower vase, an umbrella stand, and a cabinet for cigarettes... In the steward's cabin there is a sink and draining board, and large cupboards for food, drink, cutlery and china. Water is drawn from a twenty-gallon tank on the roof, on which the luggage is also carried. The very latest refinement upon all these carefully thought-out details is the provision made for wireless and a loud-speaker.'

The double-decker reborn

Leyland's next new chassis range represented an even greater advance. The Lion and its stablemates of 1925 had taken the design of the motor bus an important stage further. The new 1927 range was an even more significant development, introducing six-cylinder petrol engines as standard on bus chassis. The two main models, the Tiger and Titan, were for single and double-deck bodies respectively and were an instant success.

The Titan did more to popularise the double-decker for provinical work than any other chassis. When the TD1 was introduced at the 1927 Commercial Motor Show, it caused a minor sensation, as it was quite unlike anything that had been seen before. As a complete vehicle, the Leyland body, it weighed about 5¾tons, and the 6.8 litre petrol engine, producing 90bhp at 2,000rpm, proved more than adequate.

The bodywork represented a marked advance, with its distinctive 'piano-front', and it was particularly significant in being the first successfully to employ the lowbridge arrangement with sunken upper deck gangway, a layout that lasted for 40 years until superseded by the Lodekka and its imitators, and the rear-engined chassis. By 1929 many Titan TD1s were being fitted with enclosed-staircase bodies, but some operators continued to specify open stairs. The lowbridge Titan was the standard model until the Hybridge model was introduced in 1930.

One of Leyland's advertising slogans of the late 1920s was 'Bury your tram with a Titan'. There can be no doubt that many municipalities did just that, as the TD1 offered the first serious alternative to the ubiquitous tramcar. The Titan, too, helped many people to overcome their natural suspicion of double-deck buses, as the low centre of gravity inspired the confidence needed, particularly when the Titans were widely used on rural and interurban routes.

It is difficult to appreciate the impact of the Titan on the public, but a contemporary extract from the *SMT Magazine* helps to capture some of the enthusiastic reactions:

'The double-decker is not entirely a novelty to Edinburgh district. You will remember that before the war a bus of the type was put on by the SMT, but the top deck was uncovered, and as the war did nothing to

Left: **Traffic jams are nothing new — this was Fleet Street, London in 1924, during the British Empire Exhibition, with General K and NS type buses much in evidence.**

Below: **Four of these AEC 411s were introduced on Greyhound's pioneering Bristol-London express coach service in 1925. They had 30-seat bodies by Strachan & Brown, and one is seen at Reading.** *Foot of page:* **A fine example of the coachbuilder's (and coachpainter's) art, but already looking dated when compared with the Leyland TD1. This Hull Corporation Bristol A, with 50-seat Roe body, was new in 1928, the year after the trend-setting TD1 was introduced.**

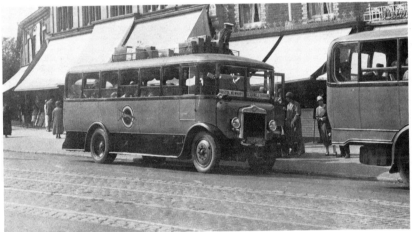

Two of Leyland's best-remembered products of the 1920s, the Titan TD1 and Lion PLSC1. These two preserved examples, seen on the annual Trans-Pennine Run, were new in 1929 and 1927 respectively to Bolton Corporation and Blythe & Berwick, Bradford. *Below:* Rear view of a Titan TD1, showing the sunken upstairs gangway, to achieve its 13ft overall height, and the outside staircase.

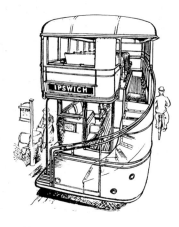

improve the prevailing weather, the exposed upper deck did not survive the climatic test. There have been wonderful developments in motor vehicles since those days, both in regard to engine perfection and coachwork comfort. The 'Titan' represents up to date, so far as public transport facilities for ordinary passenger routes are concerned, the last word in both respects. Similarly, it is throughout a Leyland job. Many original features are introduced, each one of which strengthens the impression of the amount of careful thought and extensive experiment that has gone to produce the maximum of comfort for passengers and the fullest assurance of safety.

'The 'Titan' has an extremely low centre of gravity by virtue of which it is possible to 'cant' it over at an angle of fifty degrees without upsetting. When one realises that the angle of the steepest hill from Edinburgh is only a matter of ten, the complete safety of the new bus becomes obvious. There is accommodation for fifty-one passengers, which is about twenty more than on the ordinary single-decker bus which the SMT have popularised in the Edinburgh district in recent years.

'There is one special reason why, in my opinion, the 'Titan' will speedily challenge that popularity. The height of the vehicle enables a splendid view of the countryside to be obtained from the top deck. In the course

of our run I was delighted to find new vistas and delightful glimpses opened up which hitherto had been hidden from view by high walls when I was either a pedestrian or an occupant of a low vehicle.

'The height of the 'Titan', while it gives everything that can be wanted from the point of view of appreciating the scenery through which one is passing, is only thirteen feet over all, which is approximately three feet lower than the standard tramcar. It is thus possible and safe for the bus to run on routes where there are low bridges or other obstructions. This test, as a matter of fact, will not be imposed in early history of the 'Titan', because the routes upon which it will at first run are those in Gorebridge and Balerno directions. The total length is twenty-four feet nine inches, which is rather more than three feet less than the modern single-decker, while six-wheelers are about thirty feet long, The relative shortness of the vehicle naturally makes it popular with bus operators.

'The dynamically-balanced six-cylinder engine explains the absence of vibration at all speeds. The springing, supplemented by hydraulic shock absorbers on both sides, is exceptionally smooth, and the four-wheel brakes, operated by a vacuum cylinder, have a smooth progressive action, and are extremely powerful. Externally the 'Titan' has a handsome and impressive appearance. Internally it suggests and provides the utmost comfort. An interesting novelty on the top deck is that the finely-upholstered seats are all at one side, access not being from a central passage but from a sunk side passage, which allows passengers to proceed more or less erect to their seats without danger of a bump on the head.'

Without any doubt the 1920s, can be regarded as the principal formative period of the bus industry as it is today.

It is remembered as an exciting period, but one whose excesses inevitably led to new controls, and altogether more responsible attitude to public service.

Some statistics dramatically illustrate the rise of the bus in the 1920s. In 1921 there were 48 bus-operating municipalities, with 649 buses carrying 74 million passengers; by 1930 there were 100, with 4,737 buses carrying 823 million passengers. Two company fleets which grew up in the ten years after the war were United, with a far-flung empire in eastern England, and SMT, operating mainly in central and south-east Scotland. United had 64 buses in 1919, and 619 in 1928. SMT operated 1,040,000 vehicle miles in 1919, and 10,500,000 in 1928. Dramatic growth indeed.

The first example of the unorthodox side-engined AEC Q double-decker on loan in 1933 to Birmingham Corporation, who later bought it. The 60-seat Park Royal body featured remarkably advanced styling features, particularly when it is recalled that this bus was built only five years after the Hull Bristol on page 39.

A Great Improvement in These Modern Times

1929–1939

If the years to 1918 were the bus industry's rather unsteady childhood and the 1920s its wild and mis-spent youth, then the 1930s, must represent its coming-of-age. It is convenient to include 1929 with the 1930s, for many of the events of that year had an important effect on the years that followed. The legislation of the time changed the whole face of the bus industry; it affected the services, tours and vehicles of every operator, large and small, and created a structure that remained basically unchanged for many years. The buses of the late 1930s had reached a particularly high standard; as events turned out, this was just as well, for they were called on to render much longer and more strenuous service than could ever have been foreseen.

In the last chapter we saw how the railways, in poor condition after World War I, were ill-equipped to deal with competition from the motor-bus, particularly after 1925 when the lower-built proper bus chassis made longer-distance bus and coach travel a truly practical propostition. The railways fought hard and were rewarded in 1928 with the granting to them of road transport powers. Wisely they chose mainly to buy into existing bus companies, in preference to competing directly. They purchased shares in companies which belonged to the groups which even then were emerging from the plethora of operators that had appeared in the 1920s. There were inevitable clashes between the bus managers and their new railway colleagues. W J Crosland-Taylor, one of the founders of the Chester-based Crosville company, recalled that 'individual railway officers were very acceptable, but they had been brought up on tradition, whereas we had been brought up on expediency'.

The important bus fleets of 1929 were the survivors of the cut-throat competition, the firms which had displayed better business sense and consolidated their position by acquiring their weaker brothers. There was the British Electric Traction group of companies, which had developed bus services in association with its many tramway interests throughout Britain. The BET had also initiated bus services through its associate, British Automobile Traction. Thomas Tilling Ltd., already encountered as a pioneer London bus operator, had been spreading its wings, and in 1928 Tilling & British Automobile Traction was formed,

controlling a number of important undertakings. There were other, smaller, groups, like Balfour Beatty and Provincial, and there was National Omnibus & Transport, successor to Thomas Clarkson's London firm. In Scotland there was no real group structure, but there were several larger, responsible firms which were brought together under a reconstituted SMT company.

Things were rather different in Northern Ireland. Unregulated competition continued well into the 1930s and created serious problems for the bus and railway companies. The solution was the Road and Railways Transport Act, passed in 1935, legislation which gave the country a properly co-ordinated transport system, and the most obvious result was the Northern Ireland Road Transport Board, set up in 1935 to acquire all road passenger and freight operators. In all, 65 bus and coach operators passed in to the new Board, including larger firms like the Belfast Omnibus Company, H. M. S. Catherwood Ltd., Great Northern Railway (Ireland), LMS (Northern Counties Committee) and Belfast & County Down Railway Company. A number of these operators obviously had railway roots, for the granting of road transport powers had led to direct operation by the railway companies, and road/rail co-ordination was clearly the intention.

In Eire there were three main bus operators; the Great Southern Railways, Dublin United Tramways and Great Northern Railway (Ireland). GSR was formed in 1924 by merging all the railway companies with rail services wholly in the Free State, and in 1927 GSR reached an agreement with the Irish Omnibus Company whereby IOC ran buses for GSR; in 1934 GSR took over the IOC bus services. Dublin United was originally a tramway company, but became increasingly bus-minded to combat competition from independents. The Great Northern Railway, with services on both sides of the border, was more of a problem, and continued to go its own way long after the legislation of the 1940s which created the Ulster Transport Authority and Coras Iompair Eireann.

In the re-formed BET, Tilling and SMT Groups, strengthened by railway capital, we can see the embryo National Bus Company and Scottish Bus Group of today. New companies appeared in the 1930s as local

An oil-engined 1933 AEC Regal 4
of the Dublin United fleet, with a
DUT body, at O'Connell Bridge in
1935. The bus on the left is an
Albion Valkyrie of the General
Omnibus company.

firms were merged, and the Groups embarked on a policy of consolidation, where old rivalries started to disappear and area agreements defined spheres of operation. All of this allowed the bus companies to get on with the serious business of running buses and the Government made their lives easier with the 1930 Road Traffic Act — though at the time not everyone agreed.

The Road Traffic Act was an essentially extensive piece of legislation. It introduced a national system of route licensing, controlled by Traffic Commissioners, each with responsibility for all public service vehicles in newly-created Traffic Areas. Road service licences were required for all psvs on stage carriage and express carriage services and these vehicles had to carry a current Certificate of Fitness. At the same time, the Act laid down new maximum length limits for psvs; 27ft 6in for four-wheel single-deckers; 26ft for four-wheel double-deckers, and 30ft for six-wheel single and double-deckers. This tidied up the varied regulations which applied in different parts of Britain.

It took some time before the Road Traffic Act could take proper effect, particularly when road service licences were concerned. Rival operators fought in the Traffic Courts to convince the Commissioners of their 'right' to hold the licence for certain routes and it wasn't always a case of first come, first served. For the first few years of the 1930s the battle for passengers transferred from the streets to the Traffic Courts; then, as now, anyone with an objection to a road service licence could state his case in the Courts.

New models and new developments

All this activity had no immediate effect on the design of the motor bus. The rationalised vehicle dimensions allowed makers to bring their chassis ranges into line and there was an increased demand from the newly-reconstituted bus companies — often replacements for older vehicles which failed their Certificate of Fitness examination.

Leyland had taken the lead in the 1920s with their trend-setting Lion, Tiger and Titan ranges, and now their competitors were striving to catch up. The man who was largely responsible for Leyland's dominant position was G J Rackham, the company's chief engineer. Rackham had started at Walthamstow in Vanguard days and had subsequently been involved in the London General B type. He left AEC in 1916 and in 1922 became chief engineer with the Yellow Coach & Truck company in Chicago. He returned to Britain when he joined Leyland in 1926 and lost no time in evolving the Tiger/Titan range, a fact which had not gone unnoticed by AEC, who managed to lure him down to Southall in 1928. The first fruit of this association was the 1928 AEC Reliance chassis, based on the ADC 426 model, but with a six-cylinder engine. The Reliance was really a stopgap, albeit a successful one, while Rackham developed the first versions of AEC's best-remembered models, the Regal and Regent.

The first examples of the new models used basically the same engine as the Reliance, a six-cylinder overhead-camshaft petrol unit, with a swept volume of 6.1 litres. A single-plate clutch was fitted, with a sliding mesh gearbox. The single-deck Regal and double-deck Regent were immediately successful, so much so that by 1942 some 3,500 Regals and 7,000 Regents had been built. Many of these were for London use, as we shall see

Two petrol-engined AEC Regents of the Cheltenham District fleet, with Weymann 54-seat bodies, outside Cheltenham Boys College in 1935.

later, but it is interesting to note that these models were an independent venture by AEC, without any involvement by London General.

Daimler also introduced a new model after the break-up of ADC. Again it was based on an ADC model, the 423, but the new Daimler CF6 introduced a 5.76litre six-cylinder sleeve valve engine. Daimler had preferred sleeve valve to poppet valve engines since 1909 and had actually introduced a six-cylinder engine to its passenger range in 1926. The CF6 sold well, around 600 between 1929 and 1931, but the finely-engineered sleeve valve engines had their shortcomings, as Clem Preece recalled in *Wheels to the West:*

'The special Daimler sleeve valve engine was a wonderful job in theory with white-metal lined steel sleeves, separate cylinder heads and all sorts of incredible rubber joints and pipe work. The trouble was, that if only one rubber joint were to fail and the cooling water level dropped, the white-metal sleeve lining would melt and the engine quickly become a dead loss. I fear we quickly showed the Daimler engineers that, for our sort of work, robustness came before mechanical perfection'.

Another popular single-deck chassis at the time was the Gilford, assembled in High Wycombe. Gilford was not strictly a manufacturer — the firm simply assembled parts built by other companies — but it did produce a number of good passenger models. Most Gilfords were used for coach work,

and the combination of light chassis and lively engine was ideal for this. Gilford's 1929 model was the 168, offered in both normal control (168SD) and forward control (168OT) versions, and powered by the American-built Lycoming 6litre petrol engine. The Gilford company was declared bankrupt in 1936, the combined result of a number of factors. The new company groupings absorbed many of Gilford's old customers; many of those that survived had bought vehicles on hire purchase and were slow in making repayments. There were also two remarkable front wheel drive buses, a single-decker and a double-decker, exhibited at the Olympia Show in 1931. The adoption of front wheel drive kept the height of the double-decker down to a phenomenal 12ft 11in, but the two buses, which had opposed-piston six-cylinder two-stroke Junkers oil engines, were probably just too advanced for the resources of Gilford, a company which, in spite of its short lifespan — just over a decade — is still fondly remembered today.

Two of the most important technical developments of the 1930s are still very much with us today, for the development and acceptance of the diesel engine and the epicyclic gearbox belong to this decade. The heavy oil engine, offering economy in fuel with a high torque at low speeds, was clearly ideal for passenger work and several concerns were conducting their own experiments in the later 1920s. The independent bus and coach operator Barton had experimentally fitted an oil engine into a Lancia chassis in 1928, while in Germany the truck and bus builders MAN had

Passengers board a 1929
Newcastle Corporation AEC
Regent with a 52-seat Hall Lewis
body at Haymarket. The inset
view shows one of the same
vehicles on an express service.

The popular 168 O.T. Gilford. This type of chassis can be supplied for either bus or coachwork. Here is shown a 32-seater Gilford Coach, the well-known Wycombe de Luxe type.

Essentials Only

We know Operators purchase Gilford Vehicles as a means to an end. That is why essentials, and essentials only, are embodied in Gilford design. That is why Gilford Vehicles are the essence of efficient simplicity, durability, and instant accessibility.

Gilford
'THE PROVED SIX'

GILFORD MOTOR Co., Ltd., HOLLOWAY, LONDON, N.

The Gilford was a popular coach chassis of the 1930s; the virtues of 'efficient simplicity, durability, and instant accessibility' vaunted in this 1932 advert unhappily did not hold true for Gilford, for the firm was declared bankrupt in 1936.

introduced a 5litre oil engine at the 1924 Berlin Motor Show. In Britain the turning-point came in 1928 when Gardner introduced its 4L2 and 6L2 direct injection engines for marine use. Crossley, the Manchester-based private car builder which had only entered the passenger market in 1928, fitted Gardner 6L2 units in experimental Condor double-deckers which were supplied to Leeds and Manchester Corporations in 1930. In the same year Sheffield Corporation introduced a Benz-engined Karrier oiler and Barton fitted a Gardner 4L2 in one of their buses.

Crossley did much to put the diesel engine on the map, competing with AEC who also saw the benefits. AEC developed its own diesel units, but Crossley and many other builders over the subsequent years offered Gardner engines from the 4LW/5LW/6LW range introduced for road vehicles in 1931. Other builders were slower off the mark, but as sales of diesels increased — municipalities were particularly keen customers — they developed their own oil engines, or offered proprietary makes. Leyland was slow in introducing its 8.6litre diesel, which did not appear until 1933, but a large order from the SMT Group, for engines to convert existing petrol vehicles, was a welcome shot in the arm, not only for Leyland, but for the diesel engine. The SMT Group was probably the first wholehearted convert and others quickly followed suit, so that by 1934 most new heavy-duty psvs had diesels, except for some coaches for independents, and for larger firms like Ribble and Southdown; some of the 'refined' seaside resorts continued to favour the essentially quieter petrol engine.

The preselective Wilson gearbox appeared in 1930, first in Daimler private cars and, almost immediately, in Daimler passenger vehicles. This effective transmission system allowed the driver to select a gear at any time using a hand lever, with a foot pedal to effect the actual change. The inherent smoothness, together with the fact that the driver's hands could both be on the steering wheel when necessary attracted many operators, particularly those with busy town work. London General was obviously interested and bought three of Daimler's new CH6 model. The Wilson gearbox clearly impressed London and although no more Daimlers were bought the transmission system was to be London's standard for many years. Leyland's answer was the Lysholm-Smith torque convertor, offered in its chassis from 1933. Buses thus fitted carried the words 'Gearless Bus' on their radiators, for this was almost a fully-automatic system, with no clutch pedal and a lever which had to be used to engage direct drive above about 20mph. A number of operators specified the 'Gearless' Leylands, but the system was not completely efficient and never achieved the wide acceptance of the Wilson preselector.

During the 1930s, vehicle development was steady, if normally undramatic. There were some remarkably advanced models, but none sold in spectacular numbers. It was a period of gradual improvement and it is interesting to follow one range of chassis through its production life and note the modifications. Leyland's TD range illustrates these changes most clearly; not only was it built from 1927 right through to 1942, but Leyland also altered the type designation as each change was introduced, so that it is easier to pinpoint the developments. Starting with the 1927 TD1 model as a base, it was succeeded by the TD2 (1932) with fully-floating rear axle, triple-servo brakes and a bigger 7.6litre petrol engine. The TD3 (1933) introduced the choice of petrol or diesel engines and a more compact front end arrangement. There was also the TD3c, with torque convertor; all subsequent models with this transmission also had the 'c' suffix. The replacement TD4 (1935) had vacuum-hydraulic brakes and constant mesh, rather than sliding mesh, gearbox. The TD5 (1937) had worm and nut steering and modifications to the frame. It was succeeded by two models, the TD6c (1938) and the TD7 (1939). The TD6c was peculiar to Birmingham City Transport, with torque convertor, but the TD7 which followed it included many common features, like fully-flexible engine mountings and a shorter wheelbase. There was to have been a TD8 model, announced late in 1941, but by then Britain was at war and Leyland's resources were employed in other directions.

The Leyland Titan and AEC Regent were by far the most successful of the double-deckers of the 1930s, introducing, and in some cases reintroducing, double-deck vehicles on routes outside purely urban areas. The Titan and Regent were popular with municipal, company and independent operators, while some of the contemporary models settled into more specialised slots. Double-deckers based on chassis like the Albion Venturer, Crossley Condor, Dennis Lance and Guy Arab all had their faithful supporters, though they were by no means as widespread as the Leylands and AECs. Two double-deck chassis makers which did become more familiar were Bristol and Daimler. The Bristol Tramways & Carriage Company had actually built some bus chassis as early as 1908, but it was not until 1913 that regular production commenced. Initially chassis were built primarily for the operating company, but soon other operators were buying Bristols. In 1932 Bristol became associated with the.Tilling Group and started to supply a good proportion of the Group's vehicle requirements, while still competing for outside business. Bristol's first modern double-deck chassis was the G type of 1932, originally with a 7.25 litre petrol engine, and from 1933 with Gardner's 7litre 5LW engine and also with a new constant mesh gearbox.

Daimler's best-remembered pre-war double-deck range also used Gardner diesel engines. The first Daimler COG5s appeared in 1933, but full production really started the next year and in 1935 the first COG6s appeared, using the 6LW unit rather than the 5LW. The Daimler CO series chassis were built as single-deckers and double-deckers, and while all had Wilson preselector gearboxes, most, though not all, were fitted with Gardner engines. The COG5 double-decker was the best seller in the range and at one time Birmingham City Transport had around 800 in its fleet.

The double-decker of the 1930s brought together all the design advances of the 1920s, but it is easy to forget that some of the older ideas lingered on. P. M. A. Thomas, in his review of 1930 coachwork in *Bus and Coach*, observed:

'Not a single open double-decker was shown at Olympia, but this does not mean that this type of vehicle is extinct. On the contrary, there is still a demand for the open upper deck, and Hall, Lewis, for one, produced just before the show a particularly pleasing body of this pattern, the design of which I am told,

has been registered. In appearance it resembles a modern enclosed double-decker with the canopy and upper deck windows removed but with the stairway still enclosed from behind. Wooden seats with spring bottoms and detachable waterproof cushions are fitted on the upper storey, and the upper deck extends forward over the driver and backwards over the conductor's platform, whilst the back panel is nicely curved.'

Improving the shape
The Leyland body style for the Titan TD1 had broken new ground. It was low-built and sleek, with none of the horse bus influence that had previously lingered on, even in designs like the London NS. The concept of a double-deck bus body as a rectangular box for passengers, mounted between the driver and the rear staircase and platform, gradually disappeared. The upper deck crept forward over what was originally the driver's weather canopy and forward control double-deckers, and London's eventual acceptance of glass windscreens, allowed coachbuilders to project the top deck right over the driver's cab. At the back, the staircase and platform were soon enclosed within the body and the 'traditional' British double-decker had taken shape. The low build of the new chassis allowed the designers to evolve sleeker lines and some of the most distinguished body styles of all time emerged from the 1930s.

Some builders tried a bit too hard. In an era when streamlining was the rage, some designers tried to apply aerodynamic principles to the double-deck bus, but with little lasting success, though they did

An early oiler — an AEC Regal with two-door Harrington coach body, delivered in 1933 for the Grey-Green fleet of George Ewer & Co. Ltd. *Below:* The virtues of the AEC are extolled in this 1933 advert.

contribute something towards cleaner lines. Towards the end of the 1930s some significant designs appeared. At the 1937 Commercial Motor Show, the Leeds bodybuilder Roe exhibited an AEC Regent for Leeds City Transport with a four-bay window layout which foreshadowed many designs of 10-15 years later. In 1938 Leyland introduced a modified version of its standard double-deck body, which was probably one of the most pleasing designs of all time.

As the popularity of the double-decker increased, some operators evolved their own distinctive body designs and bodybuilders throughout the country were happy to build them. It was quite possible to find buses based on the same chassis, with bodies by the same builder, looking totally different. The bigger operators, who placed sizeable orders, were the ones with the most distinctive styles; smaller operators could only expect minor modifications to an otherwise standard design.

Single-deck buses were probably more standardised. There was certainly a wide variety of designs, but these were peculiar to the main operating groups rather than to individual operators. The Tilling, BET and SMT Groups all had been evolving body layouts and features suited to their operations and they also had their own favoured bodybuilders. Tilling had Eastern Counties, the former United bodyshops at Lowestoft, which was to become a separate subsidiary of the group in 1936 as Eastern Coach Works. Lowestoft-built bodies became increasingly common in Tilling fleets, usually on Bristol chassis, which again were controlled within the Group, but they were not restricted, and many operators with no Tilling connections continued to buy ECW bodies until nationalisation in 1948 prevented them.

Not all BET-controlled fleets specified the BET Federation designs which became familiar in the 1930s; some stuck to their own styles, but a faithful group toed the party line. BET did not have the manufacturing ties of the Tilling Group. They usually used AEC, Albion, Daimler, Dennis and Leyland chassis, with bodies — often near-identical — by builders like Brush, Roe, Weymann — and even ECW.

The SMT Group had its own body supplier. The Falkirk-based Alexanders fleet had started building bus bodies for its own use in 1924 and the other SMT companies started to use its capacity from the early 1930s. The Group's requirements kept the Alexander coachworks busy and although there were isolated cases of 'outside' bodies being built, the majority of the output was

Three of the double-deck chassis types of the 1930s which were less universally popular than the familiar AECs, Bristols, Daimlers and Leylands. *Top:* **A 1932 Dennis Lance II of the Leeds Corporation fleet, with a Roe 52-seat body, seen in Bradford in 1938.** *Above:* **A fascinating period view of Birmingham in 1936, with a Corporation Morris-Commercial Imperial of 1933, which carried Metro-Cammell 50-seat bodywork.** *Right:* **One of Manchester Corporation's large fleet of locally-built Crossleys, this 1934 Mancunian had a Crossley 56-seat body.**

for SMT fleets until Alexander remained independent when the SMT Group was nationalised in 1949. In fact, the output was not enough to satisfy all SMT's needs and other bodybuilders, particularly Leyland, were widely used.

The standardised bodywork of the 1930s was mainly to be found on service buses and service coaches. Luxury touring coaches were much more varied, even for the company fleets, and the coachbuilders tended to build bespoke vehicles to suit individual preferences. There was often a basic similarity in the body construction, but the final trim and styling was a matter of individual taste.

At first, coach bodies were based on bus shells, suitably refined with external mouldings and internal decoration, but soon definite 'coach' shapes started to appear. At a time when the railway companies and car manufacturers were 'discovering' streamlining, the coachbuilders kept face by producing some quite remarkable coach bodies, often one-off jobs for Commercial Motor Shows, that were never repeated. It was also a time for gimmickry and sleeper coaches, radio coaches and observation coaches appeared on the roads; more usefully, some coaches had kitchens and toilets. Most of the novelty features were fairly short-lived, and gradually more emphasis was placed on passenger comfort, resulting in plushly-finished interiors, with quilted roofs, veneered wood facings and discreetly-curtained windows.

The combination of better coaches, railway capital and more paid holidays created a boom in coach touring and particularly in express coach travel, and during the 1930s many significant developments resulted from this. In 1932 London's Victoria Coach Station was opened and in its first operational year more than 5million passengers used it. In Cheltenham, St Margaret's Coach Station had become the 'Clapham Junction of the Coachways', an important interchange point for coach travellers from many parts of Britain. Cheltenham was the focal point of Associated Motorways, a voluntary pooling agreement, initially between six of the bigger coach operators — Black & White, Elliott Bros (Royal Blue), Greyhound, Midland Red, Red & White and United Counties. This sensible move was very much to the public's benefit, and simplified licensing procedures for the operators. With a certain justification Royal Blue timetable leaflets at the time included these aims, under the heading 'What Royal Blue Service Stands For':

Typical of Tilling group double-deck purchases in the late 1930s, a 1939 Bristol K5G with Eastern Coach Works lowbridge body, for the United fleet.

'We have but three axioms, your safety, your comfort and your convenience; to obtain them we spare no effort. Our coaches are the finest we can obtain! They and their drivers are licensed by the Traffic Commissioners through whose areas they pass, and may therefore be taken to be absolutely safe. The work of cleaning and maintaining the coaches never ceases night or day.

The result we leave to your judgement as an experienced traveller.

British all through — and proud of it.'

We have so far considered the heavy duty vehicles of the 1930s, the often-similar single- and double-deck chassis with their six-cylinder engines, petrol at first but increasingly diesel as the decade went on. Not everyone needed or wanted these chassis. There was a faction which saw a niche for lighter-weight, though full-size, single-deckers, requiring only a small four-cylinder engine, hence designs like the AEC Regal 4 and Leyland Lion.

Farther down the size scale, there was still a steady demand for small-capacity normal control chassis. Albion, Commer, Dennis, Gilford and Guy were just some of the bigger builders which also offered small bus chassis, but a newcomer to the bus business was to change all that. This new rival was a car manufacturer.

Vauxhall's somewhat late entry into the psv chassis field in 1931 was undoubtedly influenced by American competition. Since much of this competition was from GMC and Chevrolet, which, like Vauxhall, were part of the General Motors empire, it was

A late delivery to the once-sizeable GWR bus fleet — a 1930 Thornycroft A2 with 15-seat coach body, showing the hood folded back.

Birmingham Corporation built up a large fleet of Daimler COG5 double-deckers during the later part of the 1930s. This 1935 example had Birmingham Railway Carriage & Wagon 54–seat bodywork.

really only cashing in, rather than fighting it. The vehicle which eventually appeared was called Bedford, and the first Bedford WHB bus chassis was completed in July 1931 and delivered to a Bedfordshire operator at the end of August. The WHB was a small normal control chassis, with a six-cylinder 3.18litre petrol engine, while the WLB, introduced at the same time, was a longer-wheelbase version, mechanically similar under the bonnet. The WLB was an instant success, and nearly 1,900 were built in its four-year production run. It was succeeded by the WTB in 1935, a more refined approach to the constant demand for a small and economical coach, which sold over 3,000 chassis in four years. The WTB's successor, the OB, appeared in 1939, but the war prevented production from really getting under way, though the OB will reappear in the next two chapters. In the 1930s, however, Bedford really established a strong lead in the small bus and coach market, and statistics dramatically illustrate the company's growth. In 1934, 49 per cent of all vehicles in the 20-seat range were Bedfords, while in 1936 50 per cent of all registrations in the 15-26-seat class could be claimed; this figure had risen to 70 per cent in 1938.

Original thoughts

Not all of the buses of the period could be typecast quite so easily. There were manufacturers less prepared to accept that the motor bus of the 1930s — which admittedly represented a tremendous advance on its 1920s counterpart — had reached the peak of its development. For a number of years, as the bus grew in sophistication, the engine had stayed firmly at the front. Then AEC and London General started investigating the possibilities of re-siting the engine and came up with the AEC Q with its engine mounted on the offside, behind the front axle, which was itself set back from the extreme front to allow, in certain cases, a front entrance ahead of the axle.

The *AEC Gazette* for November 1932 commented:

'Many London readers of this journal will probably have seen the Q bus put on the Liverpool Street-Shepherd's Bush service by the London General Omnibus Co Ltd, some few weeks ago. And with those who have so far only seen pictures of this mystery bus, built by AEC at its Southall works, in the daily Press and one or two trade papers they will be speculating upon the constructional details of the chassis effectively hidden by the bodywork. It has its engine on the offside immediately behind the driver. So much may be gleaned by any intelligent observer.'

London General Q1 was introduced in 1932. It was followed by 233 other single-deckers and five double-deckers, delivered to London Transport in the 1934-1936 period.

The Q was built mainly in single-deck form, as a basis for buses and coaches. Royal Blue had four fine AEC Q coaches, and Clem Preece recalls them in *Wheels to the West:*

'This Q type was years ahead of its time and could run today against the most modern types without causing comment. However when we tried it out it caused a tremendous sensation — the driver actually sat with the passengers! Added to this it had no bonnet! The engine was on the offside! What is more it rode like a Rolls-Royce. People literally asked to travel on it and were prepared to adjust their times to do so. However, it had certain inherent deficiencies and it died for being ahead of its time'.

There were double-deck Qs too, fewer in number, where the engine fitted neatly under the stairs. The Q was relatively successful — considering its then revolutionary layout — and in all some 350 chassis were built, but it went out of production in 1937, presumably while AEC was perfecting a true underfloor-engined chassis.

The AEC Q was not the only side-engined chassis to appear in Britain. In 1933 Northern General, operating on Tyneside and in County Durham, introduced its first SE6 chassis, featuring a side-mounted Hercules petrol engine and, unlike the Q, a three-axle layout, the only means at the time to achieve a 30ft vehicle. There had been one six-wheel Q, but the SE6 was produced in fairly large numbers. There was also a more normal two-axle variant, the SE4, built in 1936/1938, using an AEC engine.

Oddly, it was operators rather than manufacturers who were setting the pace. Midland Red, by then one of the largest of the English company operators, had started building vehicles in 1923, mainly for its own use. The company's brilliant and energetic chief engineer, L G Wyndham Shire, had designed a series of single-deckers which were technically advanced and ideally suited to Midland Red's requirements. Large numbers were built for Midland Red, and for other fleets in the BET Group, and from 1931 Midland Red's SOS range also included double-deck models, the REDD and FEDD types, with rear and forward entrances respectively, Shire was constantly experimenting and a prototype rear-engined vehicle appeared in 1935, followed by three others in 1936; these had transversely-mounted petrol engines, coupled to Daimler fluid flywheels and Cotal epicyclic gearboxes. In 1941-1944 all four were rebuilt with horizontal underfloor engines, prototypes of a large postwar fleet.

A variation on the front engine theme was the Maudslay SF40, introduced in 1935, with a set-back front axle and front entrance alongside the driver — a layout that only really found favour a quarter of a century later. The SF40 enabled 40 seats to be fitted in a 27ft 6in bus. Initially the 4-cylinder Maudslay 5.34litre petrol engine was standard, but Gardner 4LW and 5LW diesel options were later offered.

Büssing, the German chassis builders, did a great deal of pioneer work developing underfloor-engined buses in the 1930s. Prototypes were unveiled in 1934 and underfloor-engined single-deckers were in full production only two years later.

In Britain there was similar activity, from predictable and unpredictable sources. Leyland, while enjoying the success of its Tiger and Titan ranges, was busy juggling with engine layouts in 1937. There was a highly experimental single-decker with a transverse rear engine and rear-mounted gearbox, with single tyres all round and a set-back front axle; and there was the Gnu, a twin-steer six-wheeler which had a front engine, but could also offer a front entrance.

The opulence of the 1930s coach is captured in these views of a 1933 Leyland Tiger TS6 for the Ribble fleet. The 31-seat rear entrance coach body was also built by Leyland.

PASSENGER : " WE CAN'T SIT HERE ALL DAY, DRIVER ! WHAT ARE WE GOING TO DO ?
DRIVER (FED-UP) : " WELL, 'OW ABOUT MAKING A NICE SNOWMAN ? "

Right: **One of the problems facing early express coach passengers is summed up in this 1933 cartoon.**
Below: **Front and rear views taken at Coventry in 1934, showing a new North Western Leyland Tiger TS6 with Harrington 32-seat coach body.**

Less predictable was the development of a rear-engined E-type version of the Shelvoke & Drewry Freighter, the small-wheeled chassis which enjoyed a limited success in the 1920s/1930s, largely in service at seaside resorts. The two rear-engined SDs, ordered for the Tram-O-Car service at Worthing, were actually delivered in 1938 to Southdown, who had taken over in the meantime.

The biggest operator of them all, London Transport, apparently shared this dissatisfaction with the reliable, if technically unadventurous, chassis offered by the commerical builders. London had been the main operator of the AEC Q, in single-deck and double-deck form, and in 1937 there appeared the first TF, a Leyland Tiger FEC with an underfloor-mounted engine. This was followed in 1938 by the CR, a Leyland Cub with longitudinal rear-mounted engine. There were 49 CRs in all, little-used and largely unsuccessful machines, but the 88 TFs were happier vehicles and many lasted well into the postwar period.

It would be misleading to suggest that the main manufacturers were not working on similar projects, and it is fair to say that several of these might have appeared in the early 1940s had it not been for the war. Leyland, for instance, built one Panda chassis in 1940, which was a twin-steer six-wheeler with an underfloor-engine, and this was supplied to Alexanders in 1941. AEC built an underfloor-engined chassis for Canada in 1939, a direct predecessor of the Regal IV chassis which did not appear until 1950. A more ambitious project was the six-wheel Tilling-Stevens Successor, a 1937 underfloor-engined chassis with an eight-

cylinder engine and a seven-speed gearbox; it never really left the drawing board.

Between the wars various firms experimented with producer gas, particularly as the situation darkened in Europe. High Speed Gas (Great Britain) Ltd — a very modern-sounding title for a company formed in 1933 — was one of these firms. In 1936 the company took over the London factory of the bankrupt Gilford Motor Company and formed Gilford (HSG) Ltd; the next year the solitary Gilford HSG bus appeared, based on a Gilford CF176 chassis, modified to run on producer gas. The chassis was extensively tested in Scotland and performed impressively enough to convince Highland Transport to buy it. The chassis was modified to run on peat and a Cowieson body was fitted.

Expansion in London

Amid all this activity among the manufacturers, things were happening in London. Three new types, all based on chassis in the new AEC range, appeared in the General fleet in quick succession. There was the LT class, based on the six-wheel AEC Renown, which eventually ran to over 1,400 buses, making General by far the biggest operator of this model. The LT was built from 1929 until 1932, usually with spacious and well-appointed 56 or 60-seat bodies. At a time of experiment with engines and gearboxes, the LTs, had a confusing mixture of petrol and oil engines, crash and preselector gearboxes. Later buses had Lockheed hydraulic brakes, in place of the previous vacuum servo type. There were also 35-seat single-deck LTs and private hire coaches, classed LTC.

The code LT meant 'Long T' and the basic T was the single-deck model, based on the AEC Regal chassis. Like the Regal, the London T had a long production run and the last Ts were built in 1948, 801 buses later. The first Ts were buses built late in 1929, and as the class grew it reflected the changes in regulations, in requirements and in technical matters. Many Ts were built as express coaches for Green Line routes, while others were service buses for suburban and country services.

The third T variant was the ST (Short T), based on the AEC Regent chassis. The ST was, in effect, the four-wheel version of the LT and the two types were complementary to each other, to suit varying conditions. The 25ft-long ST was introduced in 1929 and usually had seats for 48 passengers; it was built until 1932, when the regulations were altered to permit 26ft double-deckers and higher axle weights. This change largely removed the need for six-wheel double-deckers and one new longer type, the 26ft STL, replaced both the ST and LT. The STL provided up to 60 seats and was London's standard double-deck model from 1932 to 1939. The first STLs had petrol engines and crash gearboxes, but the oil engine/preselector combination became more familiar.

On 1 July 1933, little more than six months after STL1 entered service, London's buses underwent a major upheaval.

After many years of discussion, a new all-embracing authority was formed to control passenger transport in London, the London Passenger Transport Board. Its nucleus was the London General company and it also took in the services within its area operated by its associated London General Country Services, Green Line and Overground fleets, and those of Tilling, T&BAT and 55 other operators. The new London Transport monopoly also acquired a number of tramway systems, including those of London County Council, London United and Metropolitan Electric, and various urban railway services, including those of the Underground and Metropolitan Railways.

Here was the first of the giant conurbation authorities, an immense undertaking with a vast responsibility. General's 4,500-strong bus fleet was boosted by the addition of roughly 900 vehicles from its Country and Green Line associates and another 700 buses from a variety of sources. Inevitably, the fleet was a mixed one and more than 30 different chassis makes were represented. Not all were in a good condition, but London Transport had to keep as many as possible in running order until replacements could be supplied. Add the 60 trolleybuses and 2,600 trams

inherited by the new Board, and the sheer size of the undertaking becomes apparent.

One of the problems of the formation of London Transport was the future of AEC. Lord Ashfield had been chairman of Underground Electric Railways, controlling General and AEC, and in 1929 he had approached Leyland with a view to an AEC/Leyland merger. A new firm, British Vehicles, would absorb the two firms and increase its strength with other take-overs; Leyland was to be the dominant partner, with the incentive of a share of the London bus market. The deal fell through, but in 1931 discussions restarted on a Leyland

Top: **Loading up for London. One of the fine Leyland Tiger TS7s of the SMT fleet prepares to leave Edinburgh in 1936 on the 15-hour run to London. The full-fronted Burlingham coach body had seats for 22 passengers, and toilet accommodation.** *Above:* **The first Bedford bus, a WHB model with 14-seat Waveney body, supplied in 1931 to Woodham of Melchbourne, remained in use until 1961, and is now preserved.**

The wide variety of coach designs produced in the 1930s is conveyed in these four photos of Duple products. *Top:* An AEC Q 35-seater of 1933 for the Royal Blue fleet. *Centre:* A 1935 Maudslay SF40 for Lewis of Greenwich. *Above:* A 1938 twin-steer Leyland Gnu 39-seater for the City fleet. *Right:* Bird's eye view of an earlier Royal Blue coach, a 1930 AEC Regal 33-seater, showing the sliding roof and roof luggage rack, popular features of the time.

take-over of AEC. Again the London bus market was the main attraction for Leyland, with a possible guarantee of a ten-year contract to supply 90 per cent of London's buses, but again the talks broke down, and AEC and Leyland stayed defiantly separate until 1962 when Leyland eventually acquired AEC. As it turned out, one of the conditions of the Act which created London Transport in 1933 expressly forbade the manufacture of vehicles, so AEC became a separate, independent entity. Its close links with London were not severed, however, and AEC continued to be London Transport's main chassis supplier for over 30 years, initially with a guaranteed annual purchase of 400 chassis each year for ten years.

Leyland did get a look in, though, in the 1930s. In addition to the underfloor-engined TFs and the rear-engined CRs, already mentioned, there were over 100 Leyland Cubs, medium-sized normal control single-deckers which replaced and augmented the mixed fleet of small buses absorbed in 1933. There were Leyland double-deckers too, 100 Titan TD4s supplied in 1937 with Leyland-built all-metal bodywork which was adapted to resemble the contemporary STL type.

London Transport's crowning vehicle achievement in the 1930s came right at the end of the decade. The prototype of a trend-setting new class made its debut in 1938, rather ignominiously hidden under an old open-staircase body, but the following year a new body was fitted to the chassis, which had a big 9.6litre engine, flexibly mounted, and an air pressure system to operate both the brakes and the preselective gearbox. An entirely new design of 56-seat body was introduced on the RT, more rounded, well-proportioned and better finished. The RT chassis, later to be known as the AEC

London's varied 1930s buying policy is well illustrated on this page. *Far left:* **The first of the 88 flat-engined TF types was featured in this 1938 Leyland advert. Production examples had different styling.** *Left:* **One of the earliest examples of the six wheel LT type AEC Renown, in Piccadilly in 1935. The 60-seat body was built by London General at Chiswick.** *Above:* **The four-wheel contemporary of the LT was the ST, on AEC Regent chassis. This is an early example, with General-built 49-seat body.** *Below:* **One of the famous 10T10 coaches, AEC Regals with Chiswick-built bodies for Green Line services. This 1938 example is seen at Aldgate bus station.** *Foot of page:* **An early member of the large STL family of AEC Regents, a 1934 example seen in postwar days.**

Regent Mk III, and the more modern body style which it introduced heralded a new awareness of the need to combine function and aesthetic merit.

Some people might argue that the design of the London bus reached its zenith at the end of the 1930s, but some of the Board's energies were being diverted in other directions. London Transport was not only by far the biggest bus operator in Britain; in a short time it had also built up by far the biggest trolleybus fleet in the country. The Board inherited the 61 London United trolleybuses in 1933 and in 1935 started a major conversion programme, replacing the tramway system. At its height, the London trolleybus system operated 1,800 vehicles, in no less than five counties. This was very much the golden age of the trolleybus, with 18 new systems growing up between 1930 and 1939, including some important converts like Walsall, Derby, Huddersfield, Bournemouth, Newcastle, Reading, Hull, Manchester and Belfast. With this spectacular growth, the total number of trolleybuses jumped from around 500 in 1930 to 3,000 in 1938, but there were also a few casualties among the older, smaller systems.

Decline and growth

Contrasting with the growth of the trolleybus was the continued decline of the tramcar. Over the decade 39 smaller tramway systems closed, unable to cope with the combination of increasing street traffic and outworn

A late 1930s street scene in Coventry, a city that was to suffer greatly in the conflict that was spreading across Europe. This bus, a 1935 Coventry Corporation Daimler COA6 with MCW 50-seat body, was completely destroyed in an air-raid in April 1941.

equipment. Typical of the systems was that at West Bromwich, which closed down finally in 1939. Before an earlier route closure, the local press offered this none-too-flattering memorial:

'The coming of the buses on the Bromford Lane and Spon Lane routes, which has been heralded to take place shortly, will be heartily welcomed by the travelling public. The tramcars used on these routes certainly leave a lot to be desired in the way of comfort and speedy travel, while the rails are regarded by other road users as something of a terror. A journey on the antiquated and noisy vehicles which rock and jar at every imperfection in the very imperfect rails is not a pleasant experience by any means. The cars rock in a manner which almost throws one off one's seat, and at the journey's end, one has a feeling that one has just stepped off some weird machine one finds when Mr Pat Collins pays his occasional visits to the West Bromwich fairground. Trams may have been regarded as comfortable and speedy some years ago, but travel has altered with the times and the buses will be a great improvement in these modern times'.

Not everyone would have agreed with these sentiments. Certainly not the tram passengers in Blackpool, Glasgow, Leeds, Liverpool, London, Manchester or Sunderland, where fine new trams entered service in the 1930s — big, lightweight and truly modern vehicles which provided fast, efficient and comfortable services within the essential inflexibility of the tramway. Some of these operators went on to build new and better trams right through the 1940s into the 1950s, and of course Blackpool has gone on even longer; the new trams were in many cases used on new tramway extensions, some of which were built on reserved private roadways, often giving the tram a slight edge over its motorised rivals.

Just as the motor bus and the trolleybus made great advances in the 1930s, so did the motor car. Ford managed to break the magic £100 barrier, offering a fully-equipped 8hp car for this sum; in the United States Ford could justifiably use the slogan 'Count the

Fords till the next corner.' As lower prices brought private motoring within the grasp of a wider public, there was need for more legislation to control the spread. The year 1931 saw Britain's first automatic traffic signals and in 1935 pedestrian crossings and driving tests were introduced, but Britain's roads were becoming increasingly unsuitable for the growth in traffic. Neither Britain nor the United States undertook any major roadbuilding in this depressed decade; not for them the Italian *autostrada*, built partly to relieve unemployment, or the German *autobahnen*, built with easier troop movement in mind. Germany had 800 miles of *autobahn* by 1937; it was 1971 before Britain's motorway network reached this figure.

Britain's railways regained some of their former strength in the 1930s. While on the one hand there was the start of the ongoing process of branch line closure, there was the exciting high-speed streamline era of the 'Silver Jubilee', 'Coronation' and 'Coronation Scot' trains. The railways even got involved with domestic air transport when Railway Air Services was formed in 1934 by the four main line railway companies and Imperial Airways.

The year 1939 represented one of the high points in the story of the British bus. The Road Traffic Act of 1930 had given the industry a respectable foundation and the technical developments of the decade had helped to evolve a refined and efficient breed of bus. The London RT was probably the best example but there were others.

In 1939 Coventry Corporation took a number of 60-seat double-deckers into stock. Just as the London RT anticipated the trend towards air-braked, big-engined buses, the Coventry buses were the first double-deckers with high capacity, lightweight all-metal bodies. They were Daimler COA6s with Metro-Cammell bodies, weighing only 6tons 6cwt unladen and allowing a high seating capacity within the 10½ton maximum laden weight limit imposed at the time.

Other operators were anxious to obtain higher seating capacities within the length and weight regulations of the time. Northern General had a large fleet of 38-seat AEC Regals with shortened cabs and modified controls, and the SMT Group had similarly-altered Regals and Leyland Tiger TS8s, with seats for 39 passengers.

The bus industry was well equipped for the problems of the next decade, which imposed a tremendous strain on the resources of the country; all the great advances of the 1930s meant that Britain's buses were in a very healthy state by 1939, as the nation was slowly edged towards war.

THE Leyland DOUBLE-DECKER

In this first Case History page we trace the development of the double-decker from its earliest days, using Leyland vehicles to illustrate the many advances in specification and design.

The first photograph shows a 1907 Leyland U type supplied to Todmorden in 1907, a typical product of the time with its front-mounted petrol engine, solid tyres and high-built body with rear platform and outside staircase. The second photo shows a Leviathan LG1, one of the famous Leyland 'L' range of 1925. This high-built, ungainly bus for Warrington Corporation has a fairly basic top cover, but the body represented little advance on the 1907 U type. The driver, though, had moved to a position alongside the four-cylinder petrol engine.

Amazingly, the low-built 'modern' Titan TD1 came only two years after the Leviathan, and is represented here by this example for the fleet of Yorkshire Woollen. By 1934 Leyland was offering all-metal bodywork, as on the diesel-engined Titan TD4 for Ledgard, the Yorkshire independent. Five years later Leyland's standard body had reached the attractive style shown on the Central SMT Titan TD5.

Postwar production at Leyland started with the Titan PD1 in 1946, and the Scout example shows that the body style was little different from its prewar counterpart. The bigger-engined PD2 followed in 1947, and the Leyland-built 'Farington' style body of 1950 is shown on a Caerphilly Titan. The 30ft long PD3 Titan appeared in 1956, and the forward-entrance East Lancs bodied PD3 for Bolton has an unusual full-front arrangment.

The rear-engined Leyland Atlantean chassis was introduced in 1958, and the early example shown, for Chieftain (Laurie, Hamilton) had a Metro-Cammell body. The story is brought up to date with the 1975 prototype B15 integral double-decker, described in detail on later pages.

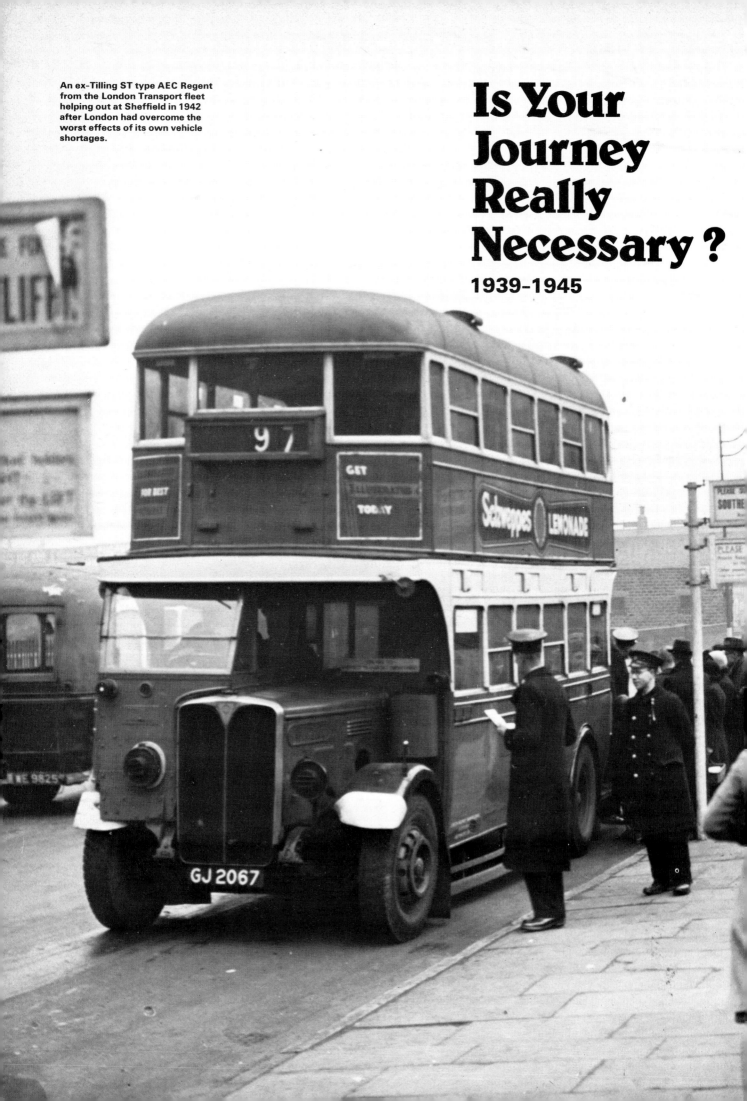

An ex-Tilling ST type AEC Regent from the London Transport fleet helping out at Sheffield in 1942 after London had overcome the worst effects of its own vehicle shortages.

Is Your Journey Really Necessary?

1939-1945

Some parts of the bus industry were well prepared for the outbreak of World War II in September 1939. As early as 1938 the Home Office had approached London Transport to see if vehicles could be made available for ambulance work in the event of the outbreak of the war so many people regarded as inevitable. LT duly obtained kits to convert its coach fleet and three days before the outbreak of hostilities it withdrew all Green Line services to carry out the conversions. Around 400 vehicles were handed over to the Ministry of Health — AEC Regals, Qs and Renowns, and Leyland FEC Tigers. Some filtered back into service, but others continued to do useful war work for the duration.

Hants & Dorset, operating on the equally vulnerable south coast of England, were also well prepared for the war. Sandbags, fire buckets and gummed paper were delivered in large quantities to company premises, and vehicle lighting was adapted to conform with the anticipated blackout regulations.

However well operators prepared for the inevitable war, there was no way that anyone could have anticipated its duration or the intensity. The immediate effects were drastic enough — fuel cuts, severe blackout restrictions and curtailed services; but things were to get very much worse before they got better.

One of the first problems encountered by the bus industry was the mass evacuation of schoolchildren and others from potential danger areas — towns and cities with heavy industry or military and naval installations — to reception areas in the safety of the country. The combined resources of the buses and the railways moved several hundred thousand children in those first, rather uncertain, days of the war. After the first few anti-climactic months, more than half the evacuees drifted back to their homes, but after concentrated bombing on London and the South Coast, there was a second blitz evacuation.

Next there were cuts in petrol and oil supplies, and enforced mileage reductions. Many operators helped to spin out their fuel supplies by cutting down the number of bus stops and often abandoned stops that involved a hill restart; parking buses in town and city centres during off-peak times cut out the dead mileage to and from depots.

Unfrozen and utility

In the early part of the war, chassis and body manufacturers continued to complete the orders they had in hand, though for service buses only; no coaches were built, as coach travel, regarded as a 'luxury', soon disappeared from the British scene. Initially,

" How about me and you girls nipping down to the seaside for the afternoon ? "

there was no obvious relaxation of the high prewar standards in many of the buses that were built in the 1939-1941 period, but production slowed after the fall of France and the Dunkirk evacuations of 1940, and as the situation worsened, the Government placed a ban on all new bus building in 1941. Spare parts and partly-built buses were 'frozen' by this move, but because of the pressing need for new buses, the manufacturers were permitted to complete and release the partly-completed buses, and buses for which parts were in stock. There were around 450 of these 'unfrozen' buses, including buses destined for export, and they were allocated to operators by the Minister of War Transport, with, if necessary, more regard to pressing needs than to fleet standardisation. The most-quoted example was the Daimler-dominated Edinburgh Corporation fleet, which found itself with a strange mixture of 'unfrozen' AECs, Bristols, Leylands and Tilling-Stevens.

While the 'unfrozen' buses helped temporarily to fill the gap for some bus operators, longer-term plans were being formulated for a new breed of vehicle, the utility bus. Orders were placed with Guy and Leyland to supply 500 double-deck chassis each, but Leyland's resources were diverted

Top: **One of London's Green Line 10T10 coaches at Reigate in its wartime role as an ambulance. They could each convey up to about ten stretcher cases.** *Above:* **Many buses and coaches were requisitioned for military use, and this contemporary Giles cartoon captures the humour of the situation.**

59

Although it was delivered in 1941, this Western National Bristol K5G with 56-seat ECW body still had the appearance of a prewar bus.

elsewhere and Guy, with fairly limited double-deck experience, was left to develop the famous utility Guy Arab, using cast iron in place of precious aluminium. The specification was straightforward, with a Gardner 5LW engine and a four-speed sliding mesh gearbox, but while most of the first 500 utility Arabs had the 5LW engine, the bigger 6LW unit became available for later deliveries.

A utility body specification was also evolved and was built by many of the leading coachbuilders in their own individual interpretations. The bodies were of composite construction (wood-framed), with seating for 56 (30/26) in the highbridge version, or 55 (27/28) in the less familiar lowbridge version; seats were usually of the simple wooden-slatted type. There was to be only one opening window on each side, on each deck and a single destination indicator at the front. Domed panels were not permitted, and in the early days windows were not permitted in the emergency exit at the rear of the top deck. To add to the appearance of undoubted austerity, the buses were often finished in plain grey or brown paint.

The equivalent single-decker was built by Bedford, a utility version of their prewar OB chassis, dubbed OWB. The choice of this normal control petrol-engined chassis was an interesting one, but with a standard utility body seating 32 passengers it provided almost the capacity of heavier single-deckers in a bus that was also suitable for rural operation. The body style on the OWB was built to a standard design by Duple, and by Mulliner, Roe and SMT. The utility Bedfords, around 3,000 in all, were allocated

to operators of all sizes, and independent, municipal and company fleets all had OWBs, in some cases squeezing many years of good service out of these useful buses.

The Daimler factories in Coventry were severely damaged by air raids in November 1940, but the company had 44 dispersal factories throughout England and North Wales, and production of aeroplane engines and the famous Daimler four-wheel-drive Scout Car was able to continue. In 1942 Daimler bus production was restarted in Wolverhampton, and 100 utility double-deck chassis were allocated to operators in 1943. The Daimler CWG5 was largely based on the successful prewar COG5 chassis, with Gardner 5LW engine and preselector gearbox.

After the first 100 chassis, AEC replaced Gardner as Daimler's wartime bus engine suppliers; the AEC 7.7litre engine was fitted to more than 1,200 Daimler CWA6s.

In all, around 1,400 utility Daimlers were built, roughly half the total of utility Guy Arabs. There was one other utility motor bus chassis, when Bristol came back on the scene with a wartime version of the prewar K model. Most were fitted with a version of the AEC 7.7litre engine and around 250 of the resulting K6A models were built in 1944 and 1945.

There was also a utility trolleybus, the W4 model, labelled either Karrier or Sunbeam, and built between 1942 and 1945. Sunbeam was an old-established company, building cars and motor buses, and, from 1931, trolleybuses. Sunbeam became part of the Rootes empire in 1935, and absorbed the production of Karrier trolleybuses the same year. Sunbeam changed hands again in 1948 when Guy Motors took over, thus completing an ironic circle, for Sydney Guy had left Sunbeam in 1914 to form his own business.

In all, some 6,700 utility buses and trolleybuses were built between 1942 and 1945. Naturally enough this was a considerable shortfall on prewar performance, but a creditable performance nonetheless in the difficult circumstances.

This was not the sum total of wartime bus building. There was a certain amount of rebodying work on older chassis; in some cases war-damaged buses were given new bodies, and in others single-deck coaches became double-deck buses, providing much-needed extra capacity.

Amazing difficulties

A great deal has been written elsewhere on the intolerable problems which bus operators faced during the war. Although the public was continually asked "Is Your Journey Really Necessary?", very often it was, and bus operators had to try to provide the necessary transport. A few examples serve to recall some of the amazing difficulties which were encountered, and usually overcome, in different parts of Britain.

Inevitably, London was the target for much of the enemy action. London Transport lost many of its vehicles in the air raids of the early war years and had to borrow buses from other operators. By the end of 1940 around 469 provincial buses were working in London. Most were double-deckers — only 83 were single-deck — and they came from 51 operators throughout Britain; the farthest travelled came from the Inverness fleet of Greigs.

The borrowed buses were returned in 1941 when the situation improved, and soon London Transport was able to lend buses to provincial towns suffering from vehicle shortages. A total of 334 ST type AEC Regents were loaned in this way.

London Transport received a reasonable allocation of new buses in the war years, though nowhere near the number it would normally expect. In addition to the 150 RTs, ordered in 1939 and delivered in 1939/40, there were 54 unfrozen buses — AEC Regents, Bristol K5Gs and Leyland Titans. From 1942 on LT took delivery of over 700 utility buses; 435 Arabs, 20 Bristol K6As, and 281 Daimler CWA6s. They were a far cry from the high quality vehicles familiar to London bus passengers, but they were serviceable machines at a time when every vehicle was valuable.

London's Green Line coach services were severely affected by the war. Most routes were suspended on 31 August 1939, when the coaches were withdrawn for conversion to ambulances, but replacement bus services were soon introduced on what had previously been coach-only sections and in 1940 Green Line routes trickled back. By September 1942 the war situation had worsened considerably and all Green Line routes were withdrawn for an annual saving of more than 11 million miles. There were no Green Line services until February 1946, but in the meantime LT had carried out a survey to discover what former Green Line passengers were doing instead. Half were simply not travelling; another 20% were using country buses; 10% central buses; under 10% railways; and a negligible number had switched to trams, trolleybuses and tubes.

Southampton was a major problem for Hants & Dorset during the war, for this important seaport also housed the main Supermarine factory, producing Spitfire aircraft. After several false alarms, the factory was eventually destroyed in

September 1940, necessitating a high-speed exodus from the area, with Hants & Dorset and Southampton Corporation buses evacuating workers to safety.

On another occasion, a dive-bomber attack on Gosport, an H&D driver recalled that 'after the all-clear sounded, I set off again in my "E-type" (a Leyland TD1) and was bowling up to the top of the Rowner Railway Arch when I saw the middle was missing. I just managed to stop in time and reversed back into a field.'

Sussex — Southdown territory — was regarded as a safe area in 1939 and thousands of children were evacuated to its town and villages. But after Dunkirk the South Coast came dramatically into the front line and the evacuees were re-evacuated. Many thousands of troops moved into the area, however, and this made great demands

Two illustrations from a 1941 SMT advertisement which listed 'Things you mustn't do in the black out'. *Above:* **'Don't dazzle the driver trying to stop him.'** *Below:* **'Don't walk out from behind the bus without looking'.**

A scene of undoubted austerity at Grays, Essex. One of three Brush-bodied lowbridge 55-seat utility Guy Arab Is supplied to Eastern National in 1942.

on Southdown, already short of vehicles and crews. The company's success in providing essential transport while also saving precious fuel is clearly illustrated by the passenger and mileage comparisons between 1939 and 1944; the total mileage dropped from 22½ million to less than 16 million in five years but in the same period passenger figures rose from 60 million to 90 million.

Much of Kent was declared a Defence Area and the East Kent bus company found itself very vulnerable to shelling, fighter-bomber aircraft and the later flying bombs. The buses themselves were often attacked by German aircraft, and the constant danger faced by the crews around Dover gave rise to the well-deserved nickname "The Busman's Malta".

Inevitably, East Kent's wartime toll was heavy. Many staff were killed or injured, three depots almost totally destroyed and many vehicles damaged, but the willing efforts of all staff ensured that the company's important contribution to the war work was a successful one.

The Royal Blue express services of Western National and Southern National were still in the midst of a typically busy summer season when the war broke out. The emphasis then switched from the predominant holiday traffic to traffic of a more essential nature. The Royal Blue services linking London, South Central and South West England were important links, but by November 1942 all had to be suspended. Replacement bus services were provided over roads not otherwise covered, and it was 1946 before express services re-started.

Wearside was a centre of shipbuilding and

heavy industry, but the recession in the North-East had meant that the Sunderland Corporation tram services did not always serve these areas which were now of vital importance. For this reason, more buses were needed in the tram-predominated fleet, and there was a proportionately high intake of utility buses. The trams played an important part, particularly as crowd-movers; there is at least one reported case of the conductress of a 62-seat tram refusing a passenger because there were already 112 aboard!

There was a huge influx of workers into the area served by Bristol Tramways for the aeroplane and other factories, and the bus fleet was stretched to the limit. To add to Bristol's problems nearly 2,000 busmen joined the Services and the company was in the midst of a replacement scheme for the Bristol trams. At first the tramway abandonment plans were postponed, but early in 1941 one of the tram depots was destroyed and later the main cable from the company's central power station was damaged, so that the end of the tramway system was artificially accelerated.

Coventry Transport entered the war like every other municipal operator. Bus and tram windows were lacquered in blue, bus roofs were painted grey in place of the normal ivory and frequencies were reduced. There was some slight bombing in August 1940, but three months later the city was the target for a savage air raid which destroyed Coventry Cathedral, reduced much of the city centre to ruins, wrecked or damaged over half the Coventry bus fleet and forced the immediate withdrawal of the remainder of the tramway system. Luckily there were

some hired buses held in reserve and these were hastily pressed into service; others were borrowed from municipalities, mainly in the North-West of England, and from London.

Faced with more than its fair share of wartime problems, Coventry Transport struggled valiantly on, helped by reasonable supplies of unfrozen and utility buses.

Gas, tanks and trams

One problem of running buses in wartime was peculiar to only a handful of operators. In October 1942, with the object of protecting fuel supplies, the Ministry of War Transport ordered 57 large British bus operators to convert 10 per cent of their fleets for gas operation. The eventual target was 2,500 gas buses, but that was never reached.

Petrol-engined buses, with their much lower compression ratio, were usually chosen for conversion, using the standard two-wheeled producer gas trailers. These had a firebox, an anthracite hopper, a water tank and a cooler, and produced gas from activated anthracite and water. The performance of gas buses was good on the flat but sluggish on hills, and operators were delighted to comply with the Government instruction to abandon the use of producer gas in September 1944.

Although bus chassis manufacture was in the hands of only Bedford, Daimler and Guy for the best part of the war, the other bus builders were equally involved in the national effort. AEC built Matador artillery tractor units, armoured cars, mine-sweeping equipment, Marshal lorries and engines for tanks. Bristol, before it returned to bus work. made shells, tank components and aircraft

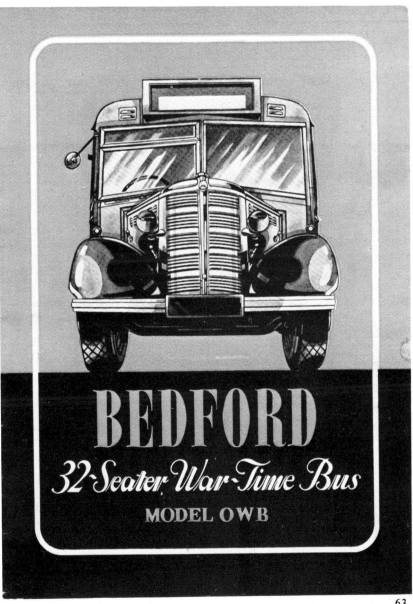

BEDFORD
32-Seater War-Time Bus
MODEL OWB

fuselages.

Leyland's massive war effort included the production of over 10,000 tank engines, over 3,000 tanks, over 7,500 high explosive bombs, over 11million incendiary bombs and over 5million 20mm shells.

Operators too played their parts. SMT, for instance, with a thriving pre-war private car business, had useful engineering and production capacity. In various factories throughout Central Scotland they produced aircraft assemblies and gun parts, assembled motor vehicles, refitted marine engines and built vehicle bodies, including utility buses on Bedford OWB chassis.

London Transport, too, made good use of its vast resources as a partner in London Aircraft Production , assembling Halifax bombers. Chrysler built the rear fuselage, Duple the nose shell, Express Motor & Body Works the inner wings and tailplane, and Park Royal the outer wings. LT built the centre section, installed the engine fuselage and front section, completed the erection and test-flew the plane. They used a new building at Aldenham, later to become an important bus overhaul works.

The war effectively cancelled out any problems of competition. As we have seen, bomb damage caused the premature

The original caption on this October 1939 photo reads: 'Although there has been some diminution of traffic and reductions in certain services, London Coastal Coaches' station, at Victoria, still presents a busy appearance. These AEC Regals maintaining Royal Blue winter timetables, are among many other Southall-built coaches working for other companies and making daily use of the station'. The coaches are 1937 Mumford-bodied 31-seaters.

Coventry, November 1940, and the remains of a 1939 Daimler COG5/60 lie among the smoking ruins of the city. Amazingly, the bus was to see further service, as it was salvaged, and rebodied in 1942.

withdrawal of two tramway systems, but some others just managed to struggle on until the end of the war. The hostilities slowed the prewar pace of tramway withdrawal, for trams often came into their own with fuel rationing. The only drawback was the tram's basic inflexibility, particularly where the tracks were damaged in air raids. Some of Coventry's trams were still standing abandoned on isolated sections of track weeks after the system's enforced abandonment.

Trolleybuses had the same advantages and disadvantages. Amazingly, one new system opened — the second last in Britain — at Cardiff in 1942. The decision to introduce trolleybuses in the Welsh capital had been taken early in 1939, and contracts had been placed.

Private motoring for other than essential purposes came to an abrupt stop early in the war, and it was to be some time before a full return to prewar levels could be made. This wartime cutback forced an extra load on to public transport.

Peace at a price

As the war situation improved some of the restrictions affecting bus operators were relaxed; blackout regulations were less stringent, and utility buses were less austere. There was also a certain amount of preparation for a resumption of peacetime production. In 1943/44 Crossley and Midland Red both had built prototypes on which their postwar models were based, and Daimler introduced a completely new bus engine, the 8.6litre CD6 unit, in 1944.

By VE Day in May 1945 Britain was counting the cost of six long years of war. The bus industry had kept going in the most difficult circumstances, coping with shortages of staff, of vehicles, of fuel, and in many cases with the wholesale destruction of depots, offices and buses. But the peace had been hard-won and the industry faced a major rebuilding task to re-attain the standards of the late 1930s. Forward planning had been forced into the limbo of an uncertain future; the travelling requirements of peacetime Britain were an unknown quantity; buses which had been bought in the early 1930s with a useful life expectancy of eight or nine years, were now running on borrowed time, and were showing their age; while the utility buses provided reliable — if basic — transport, they represented only a small proportion of the normal peacetime vehicle intake for most fleets.

The war had presented a mixed bag of problems for the bus operator, but peace was to present new problems, often with less immediate solutions.

A practical, in ungainly, solution to the fuel problem. This Barton Transport Leyland Lion LT8, one of ten supplied in 1939 with Duple 39-seat bodies, received an apparently unwieldy gasholder (*left*) and could be filled from a large main of town gas (*below*).

The more familiar form of producer gas bus towed a small trailer, which carried a firebox, anthracite hopper and water tank. This London Transport ST is seen in the West End in 1943.

65

FOLKESTONE
VIA
ASHFORD
SERVICE 10

All shoulders to the wheel in March 1946, as passengers help a 1944 Daimler CWA6/Weymann utility out of a snowdrift on the Ashford-Folkestone road.

Back to the Same Old Bus

1945-1950

An advert for the SMT Group which appeared late in 1946 summed up the feelings of many transport operators in those early postwar days. Under a photograph of a Western SMT driver, newly returned from six years' war service, the copy ran:

'He's back from the Services — back to the same old job — back to the same old bus. He might have had a brand new bus waiting for him — but new ones are needed for export too. We didn't get many replacements during war-time; we can't get many even now, and we are still short of highly skilled maintenance men. So the war-time shortage of "fit" buses still lingers on. That means we aren't running the kind of bus service we gave you pre-war, but we are all out to get enough new buses to give you service and facilities we can boast about once again!'

So the problems of wartime had given way to the new problems of peacetime. In 1945 there was a natural reaction to the strictures of the previous six years: Britain was at peace again and the British people wanted to celebrate. They had money to spend, but there was little to spend it on. The BBC Television Service returned in June 1946, but was still available to a very limited audience; the private car industry was still recovering from the pressure of war work and fuel was still rationed. The result was a tremendous growth in leisure travel, and the bus and coach industry enjoyed an unexpected boom which was to help them through these days of austerity and continued rationing.

Not that things were any easier for bus operators. There were precious few new buses to be had and most fleets contained an unhappy assortment of time-served veterans, tired after prolonged war service, and vehicles dating from the immediate prewar period, basically sound but often in need of proper overhaul. These were the lucky ones. The less fortunate operators — often those with predominantly coach fleets — had lost some or all of their vehicles to the Services in the early days of the war, and were now faced with the problem of rounding them up.

When the first new postwar buses appeared in 1945/46 they were largely similar to their immediate prewar counterparts. There were, of course, sound practical reasons for this, as the bus builders had been concentrating on everything from jeeps to planes and new design work was inevitably curtailed. But operators were glad to get hold of anything new. And that meant literally anything. Unfamiliar chassis and body makes appeared in what had once been highly-standardised fleets and there was a great spate of rebuilding and rebodying older

vehicles. But all this was aggravated by the desire to re-establish British goods in world markets and priority was given to exports for a while.

Familiar chassis like the AEC Regal, Bristol L and Leyland Tiger made their reappearance on the British market in 1946, with few major changes to their sturdy and straightforward specifications. Bedford, with the wartime OWB production behind it, bounced quickly back with the OB, which virtually cornered the market for small normal control chassis. Other smaller models appeared in 1946, the normal control Commer Commando and Guy Wolf, and the forward control Guy Vixen. Even Leyland had a stab at the lucrative market for smaller coaches with its normal control Comet range introduced in 1947, but it was most at home competing for the full-size single-deck business, where the Tiger had to fight off models like the Daimler CVD6, Dennis Lancet, Guy Arab and Maudslay Marathon. 'Full-size' at the time usually meant 27ft 6in by 7ft 6in, and in spite of the many experiments of the 1930s the engine was still firmly at the front, except in the Midland Red fleet. The Birmingham-based company had managed to get the first postwar British production underfloor-engined buses in service in 1946, with its S6 model, designed and built purely for its own use. Next came Sentinel, with the integral STC4 model, and Commer with the petrol-engined Avenger, featuring a front-mounted underfloor-engine. These were important moves, but it took the entry of the big guns and a change in the regulations affecting vehicle dimensions in 1950 to herald the real arrival of the underfloor bus.

AEC and Leyland, deadly rivals at that time, were both anxious to show their new underfloor models to the world. The first complete AEC Regal IV, with horizontally-mounted 9.6litre engine, appeared early in 1950, while the first Leyland/MCW Olympic, an integral model with horizontal 9.8litre engine, was unveiled late in 1949. Early examples of both models were only 27ft 6in long, but the 1950 change in dimensions permitted 30ft by 8ft single-deckers and the new size was eagerly adopted.

Leyland's Olympic, developed jointly with coachbuilder MCW, enjoyed only a limited success on the home market, but a much more spectacular success overseas. A separate chassis, the Leyland Royal Tiger appeared in 1950, opening the floodgates for a veritable rush of similar chassis. By September 1950, when the 15th Commercial Motor Show was opening, the AEC and Leyland models had been joined by new

underfloor models from Atkinson, Dennis
and Guy, but their successes and failures
really belong in the next chapter, as does the
undoubted success of another 1950 model,
the forward control Bedford SB which
replaced the highly successful OB model.

The demand for new buses and coaches
attracted many new names to the
coachbuilding business. Some were
commercial bodybuilders who had turned to
coaches and their efforts were often as mixed
as their origins. The magazine *Bus & Coach*
for December 1949, for instance, carried
adverts from 27 coachbuilders — and that
did not include some of the larger firms like
Burlingham, Massey, Northern Counties,
Plaxton and Roe. Many of the 27 are only
vague memories more than a quarter of a
century later — names like Crawford Prince-
Johnson, Samlesbury, Duffield, All-Weather,
Gurney Nutting and Trans-United.

There were crude attempts at streamlining
many of the coaches of the period, and often
a full-width front disguised the normal
exposed radiator, another concession to
'modernity'. But the coaches of the 1940s
which weathered best were the simpler
designs, often with direct prewar ancestry,
which came from the longer-established
builders.

Bigger engines and tin fronts

The double-decker of the 1940s had a front
engine and rear entrance, seating 56 in
highbridge form, of 53 in side-gangway
lowbridge form. It had a bigger engine than
its equivalent of a decade earlier, and while
Midland Red and Foden — and eventually
every builder — fitted tin fronts in place of
the traditional exposed radiator, few major

mechanical changes had taken place for
some years. The Bristol/ECW Lodekka
changed all that.

The Lodekka was a revolutionary new
design with a low centre of gravity to permit
normal-height central gangways in both
decks within the 'lowbridge' height of 13ft
4in. The prototype appeared in 1949 and the
Bristol Lodekka was to prove by far the most
successful low-floor double-deck design.

But in 1949, Bristol's front-line double-
deck model was the traditional K type, which
reappeared in peacetime form in 1946,
joining the postwar models from AEC,
Albion, Crossley, Guy and Leyland.

AEC's first postwar model was introduced
in 1945, designated Regent Mk II. This
straightforward chassis combined the AEC
7.7litre engine, a sliding mesh gearbox and
vacuum brakes — a standardised specification which helped many operators in their
urgent demands for new buses. A more
refined AEC double-decker, the Regent Mk
III, appeared in late 1946 when chassis
based on the trend-setting RT type of 1938
were delivered to some provincial customers.
The later provincial Regent III model was
clearly based on the RT, as originally offered
with 9.6litre engine, preselective gearbox and
air brakes, but had a quite different frontal
appearance. There were later models with
options like the sliding mesh gearbox, the
7.7litre engine and vacuum brakes.

Leyland also answered the urgent call for
new buses with a fairly basic model, the
Titan PD1, which first appeared in 1946.
This featured a new 7.4litre engine, based on
units fitted in Leyland-built tanks, and was
coupled to a constant-mesh gearbox and
vacuum brakes. As with the AEC Regent,

Another express service re-starts
— at Norwich bus station a 1939
Eastern Counties Bristol L5G with
stylish 26-seat ECW coach body
prepares to leave for London.

the PD1 was soon followed by a more refined chassis which eventually replaced it. The Leyland Titan PD2 first appeared in 1947, with a new 9.8litre engine and a synchromesh gearbox, a powerful and smooth combination that guaranteed the PD2 a long and successful lifespan.

The rugged combination of medium-powered engine, constant-mesh gearbox and vacuum brakes was widely favoured in the 1940s and 1950s, and could be found in chassis like the Albion Venturer, Bristol K, Crossley DD42, Dennis Lance, Foden PVD6 and Guy Arab III. The Gardner 5LW and 6LW engines were available on all except the Albion and Crossley chassis, while Bristol and Dennis also offered their own engines as alternatives. Daimler's postwar CV series gave customers a choice of the two Gardner engines and Daimler's own 8.6litre CD6 unit.

By 1950 the chassis manufacturers were offering further refinements in their double-deck models. Operators had found that big engines, running below full power, were economical and reliable, and even larger engines like the 10.35litre Meadows 6DC630 and the 10.6litre Daimler CD650 were introduced. The Meadows engine was available in the Guy Arab as an alternative to the more normal Gardners, but the CD650 Daimler appeared in an advanced model carrying the same designation and featuring hydraulic power-assisted operation for steering and gearchange, as well as brakes. Neither of these combinations really caught on for home market models, though, and the Gardner engine continued to find the most favour among operators.

The Midland Red company continued to go its own way as far as new double-deckers were concerned. During and after the war it had been forced to buy AECs, Daimlers, Guys and Leylands, but in 1949 the new BMMO D5 model appeared, based largely on a wartime prototype. The D5 had BMMO's 8litre engine, a constant-mesh gearbox and hydraulic brakes, and it had a full-width bonnet front concealing the radiator. Two hundred D5s were built, the second hundred with doors on the rear platform.

Return to standardisation

London Transport suffered from the same postwar problems that dogged every operator, only on a much larger scale. But London Transport ended the war in a much healthier state than the equivalent transport authorities in Berlin and Paris; there was literally no public transport running in Berlin at the end of the war, while in Paris one of the first peacetime tasks was to round up the vehicles which had been dispersed far and wide under the German occupation. London Transport, on the other hand, only lost 156 of its 6,000 buses during the war. Even so, one of the first priorities was fleet renewal and LT's prewar standardisation was abandoned in the interests of quick deliveries; but of the 746 new buses ordered for 1946, only 225 were delivered that year. There were AEC Regent IIs and Leyland Titan PD1s, and the equivalent single-deck AEC Regals and Leyland Tigers, but London Transport was anxious to take deliveries of its RT model and huge orders were placed. By the end of 1947 around 4,000 RTs were on order, but only 182 had been taken into stock. The position gradually improved and between 1947 and 1954 LT received a staggering total of 4,673 RTs; add to this the 1,631 RTLs, Leyland Titans built to London specification, and the 500 RTWs, Titans again, but 8ft wide, and the RT family eventually totalled nearly 7,000 buses — standardisation indeed!

The RT, well-designed, efficient and reliable, helped London to cope with the unexpected postwar rush of passengers, but deliveries were slow to gain momentum and there were various temporary measures to overcome this. Around 550 coaches of all shapes, sizes and ages were hired from private operators for relief work, and there were also 180 new Bristol double-deckers, intended for Tilling Group firms, which ran for a while on the London streets. The situation gradually eased, though at one stage there were more RT bodies than chassis, so the new bodies were mounted on rebuilt prewar STL chassis and classified SRT; only 160 SRTs were produced, as the chassis problem quickly improved.

There was no complacency in London, however, and plans were already in hand for the RT's successor. In the final years of the war and in early postwar years, LT was also looking at the possibilities of employing a seated conductor on double-deckers, on the pay-as-you-board principle. Several buses, STLs and trolleybuses, were experimentally converted, but without much success. Another conversion was RT97, one of the prewar RTs which had been damaged by a V1 rocket in 1944 and which reappeared with an air-operated sliding door. The same bus was totally rebuilt to re-emerge at RTC1, extensively modernised inside and out. Its sleek lines foreshadowed the RT's

replacement, introduced five years later, while inside it had an advanced heating and ventilating system, tilted-back seats and fluorescent lighting.

New controls

The changes in the economic and social climate in Britain following the war forced transport much further into the political arena. The Labour Government of 1945 inherited a country that has been described as 'morally great, but economically bankrupt', and its solution to many of the problems it faced was nationalisation. In its six-year term of office the Labour Government nationalised mines, electricity, railways, road haulage, gas, iron and steel — and some large segments of the bus industry.

Necessity had largely mothered the fusion of the four main-line railway companies into British Railways in 1948. Forced to work together in the war — with a creditable degree of success — the railways too were suffering from the war's after-effects. Nationalisation plans had been announced in 1945 and the 1947 Transport Act created the British Transport Commission. The Act came into force on 1 January 1948, and the BTC assumed immediate control of British Railways and London Transport. The old London Passenger Transport Board gave way to the new London Transport Executive, and the 1947 Act further affected the bus business in that the railway shareholdings in the many company fleets throughout Britain had automatically passed into the nationalised control of the BTC. The next logical step was the sale of the Tilling Group road transport interests to the BTC for just under £25million. Faced with a similar

A foretaste of new trends — a line of Midland Red underfloor-engined S6 buses poses at Coventry early in 1947.

situation, the SMT Group in Scotland decided that voluntary sale of its bus interests to the BTC was a sensible move, and in 1949 SMT joined Tilling in the nationalised ranks, for a price of almost £27million. The BTC bus empire was also enlarged with the acquisition of the Red & White group and of a number of smaller, but important, independent operators which helped them to gain footholds in other parts of Britain, while the nationalisation of electricity brought the Mansfield District, Midland General and Notts & Derby companies into BTC hands.

There were changes too in Northern Ireland, where the Northern Ireland Road Transport Board passed to the Ulster Transport Authority in 1948 along with the Belfast & County Down Railway and the lines formerly operated by the LMS.

The changes in the bus industry were not confined to the operating side of the bus business. Bristol's bus chassis side and Eastern Coach Works had both passed to the BTC with the Tilling sale, and their products were now restricted to nationalised fleets; in practice, the Tilling companies, always staunch Bristol/ECW users, were to buy nothing but Bristol/ECW products for more than 15 years. The Scottish Group did buy a proportion of Bristol/ECWs, but also retained its normal suppliers, like AEC, Bedford, Guy and Leyland, often with Alexander bodies, although here the situation was rather different. The Alexander coachbuilding activities were severed from the operating company upon nationalisation and a new private company was formed, handling not only Scottish Group work, but also an increasing demand from Scottish

One of the most significant postwar designs was the Bristol/ECW Lodekka, which achieved a lowbridge overall height with normal gangways on both decks. This was the prototype Lodekka 58-seater of 1949 for the Bristol company; production models had their radiators concealed behind tin fronts. The low build that allowed this is apparent in the interior view.

A product of Santus of Wigan, one of the smaller coachbuilding factories that thrived in the postwar demand for new vehicles. This Santus-bodied Maudslay Marathon III was supplied to Taylor Bros., North Shields, in 1947.

71

The London Transport RT type AEC Regent III, conceived in the late 1930s, was still giving good service into the late 1970s. This 1950 example is seen in 1973 in Whitehall.

municipal and independent fleets, and eventually from operators in England and Wales.

A group of leading manufacturers was considering an uncertain future when AEC, Albion, Dennis, Leyland and Thornycroft met in 1945 to discuss a scheme for integration, but it was Leyland — potentially one of the strongest components — which held out against the possibility of mono-polies, price maintenance and nationalisation, coming down firmly in favour of competitive enterprise.

AEC and Leyland were the most directly competitive of the heavy commercial vehicle manufacturers. Leyland was jealous of AEC's long links with London Transport which ensured AEC's near-monopoly of London's bus orders. In 1946 Leyland managed to break the monopoly and obtained a 25 per cent share of London's orders — not hugely profitable business, but regular, long-run work. This so pleased Leyland that they proclaimed in their adverts in the trade press that 'chassis and buses were now regularly leaving the Leyland factory for London at the rate of three every working day'. Leyland's position was further emphasised by a reminder that 'Leyland is the only single manufacturer of both chassis and bodywork to have supplied London with complete double-deckers'.

In spite of the intensity of their rivalry, AEC and Leyland did pool resources in 1946 to form British United Traction, a combination of their previously separate trolleybus-manufacturing interests. BUT built trolleybus chassis to both AEC and Leyland designs for many years and later diversified to supply large quantities of diesel engines for British Railway multiple units.

At the same time, AEC was busy looking

for ways to expand its empire, and in 1948 it bought over two well-respected manufacturers, Crossley and Maudslay. The enlarged company, Associated Commercial Vehicles, encompassed AEC, Crossley and Maudslay, but the Crossley and Maudslay names survived only for a few years on what were otherwise AEC chassis. There was further empire-building in 1949 when ACV acquired the bodybuilding firms Park Royal and Roe. Guy was also expanding at the time and in 1948 bought over the Sunbeam trolleybus business.

In 1949 Britain's last new trolleybus system was opened, when Glasgow Corporation added trolleybuses to its motor buses, trams and subway trains. The Glasgow trolleybus played only a small part in the large Glasgow network, during the later part of its comparatively short lifespan.

Glasgow was also demonstrating its faith in electrical traction by continuing its tramway fleet renewal. Between 1948 and 1952 it placed 100 new Cunarder trams in service and other towns were also investing heavily in the tramcar. Aberdeen, Edinburgh, Leeds and Sheffield all bought new trams in the late 1940s, but they were going against the trend, which was to continue the abandonment process of the prewar period. The total number of trams in service in Britain fell from around 6,000 in 1945 to 4,700 in 1950, following withdrawal at cen-tres like Manchester, Leicester, Southampton, Cardiff, Newcastle and Bradford.

The odds were heavily weighed against the tram in its traditional British role as a method of street transport. A few systems had built tramway extensions on reserved track, segregated from other road traffic, following the successful example of many of

the Continental tramways, but most British trams had to operate in the middle of roads that were increasingly choked with motor traffic. Add to this the poor state of much trackwork, following wartime neglect, and the high cost of a new tramcar — £10,000 as against £4,000 for a new bus — and the era of the British tram was nearing an end.

The postwar Indian Summer of the motor bus was also nearing its end. The passengers continued to flock on to the buses and for many operators 1949 and 1950 were the best-ever years for passenger loadings; Manchester Corporation, for instance, carried a record 492million passengers in 1949. But then the figures started a slow decline, as private motoring mobilised the masses and television offered an indoor alternative to theatres and cinemas. Fortunately the passenger boom and the change in the structure of the industry had placed the operators in a strong position to face the future.

Not only bus travel was threatened. The coach business, too, was changing to suit new public preferences in the express and leisure markets. The express coach network had restarted gradually after the war and initially new coaches had been low on the list of priorities. But as this changed, some fine vehicles took to the road, including a fleet of double-deck coaches for Ribble express services. Coach touring got off to an even slower start, but by 1947 some operators were actually running overseas tours — a foretaste of later holiday trends.

Private motoring really got into top gear in 1950 when petrol came off the ration — the same year the London Transport withdrew its last petrol-engined bus, when the Inter-Station Leyland Cubs reached the end of the road with LT.

Above: **Like the London RT, the Bedford OB is fondly recalled as a classic of its time. These three Greenslades coaches, with the ever-popular Duple Vista body, are seen in 1949 preparing to leave Exeter coach station for a tour of the Minehead and Lynmouth districts.**

Left: **The AEC Regent II was AEC's first, and fairly basic, postwar double-deck model. Liverpool Corporation took a batch of these Weymann-bodied examples in 1945.** *Below:* **The underfloor-engined Regal IV represented more advanced thinking from AEC. This 1949 prototype with 27ft 6in long Park Royal 40-seat body demonstrated to various operators, including London Transport.**

Greater Comfort and Added Amenities
1951–1960

A fleet of 300 of these Leyland Titan PD2/20s with ultra-lightweight MCW Orion bodies joined the Edinburgh Corporation fleet in 1954–57 to replace trams like the 1935 example on the left in Princes Street in 1954.

The operators who went into the 1950s confidently expecting the peak loadings of the 1940s were in for a rude awakening. It was certainly an eventful decade, but the private car and the television set continued to eat into passenger figures and operators had to take an urgent look at the economics of their business. The inevitable outcome was a slow start to the seemingly endless round of fare increases and service reductions and withdrawals.

But there was also a good side to the 1950s. The structure of the bus-operating industry remained fairly static; after the upheaval of nationalisation there was some minor mopping-up to achieve a neatly-organised industry. There was the nationalised BTC, controlling the Tilling, Scottish and London Transport fleets; the rival BET Group, with the rest of Britain's "company" buses; roughly 100 municipal bus fleets; and innumerable independents, ranging from the big ones, like Barton, Lancashire United and West Riding, to one-coach fleets. The main changes in the 1950s really affected the design of the bus, the first positive moves away from the basic concept developed in the late 1920s.

Firstly, though, the threats to the bus industry. In London alone the 300,000 TV sets of 1950 had grown to 2million ten years later. The growth in private motoring was equally dramatic — from 2¼million cars in 1950 to 5½million in 1960. The stay-at-home habits encouraged by television and the spread of the weekend motorist both seriously affected passenger loadings on the buses. The car also became more of a problem in urban areas, creating traffic congestion and hampering the smooth progress of public transport. The bus at least could cope after a fashion, but the essentially less flexible trams and trolleybuses faced new difficulties; this was just one of the factors which hastened their demise.

Some of the best-known tramway systems disappeared during the decade, reducing Britain's tramway population from 4,700 to just 400. Notable casualties were London (in 1952), Birmingham and Belfast (1953), Sunderland (1954), Dundee and Edinburgh (1956), Liverpool (1957), Aberdeen (1958), Leeds (1959) and Sheffield (1960). Among the trams consigned so unceremoniously to the scrapyard were relatively new — and expensive — cars with many years of good service in reserve. On the positive side, Blackpool was experimenting with trailer cars and in 1960 ordered ten trailer cars for high-capacity motor-and-trailer sets.

Activity on the trolleybus front was also fairly positive, even though Manchester Corporation reported in 1953 that the trolleybus was 'materially less efficient'. In 1954 Walsall Corporation displayed its faith in the trolleybus by introducing the first of 22 Sunbeam F4A double-deckers with Willowbrook bodies. These were 30ft long on two axles, at a time when the maximum permitted length was 27ft, and the Walsall Sunbeams anticipated the relaxed legislation of 1956. In 1958 Glasgow Corporation obtained special dispensation to buy ten 34ft 5in long single-deck trolleybuses (30ft was the legal maximum at the time). These were used for Britain's last tram-trolleybus conversion in 1958, and the route was the last outpost of the single-deck trolleybus, always a comparative rarity in Britain. Glasgow's experience with buses of this length encouraged the authorities to permit 36ft buses from 1961.

Heavyweights and lightweights

The dawn of the Elizabethan age boosted British morale, signifying the end of austerity and the start of a new era which was typified by the new Comet airliner and the conquest of Mount Everest. Bus builders seemed to get caught in this mood of infectious optimism, and their new products certainly displayed ingenuity and advanced thinking in the country's best traditions. As we have already seen, the underfloor-engined single-decker really arrived in 1950, when a whole host of new models appeared. This first generation of underfloor models had a mixed reception. Some, like the AEC, Bristol and Leyland models, sold well; most of the others attracted a small, though regular, clientele. Only the Dennis Dominant, which featured a semi-automatic Hobbs gearbox, could be called a flop, but Dennis wisely offered a more familiar package, the Lancet UF, in 1953, and this had a faithful following.

Not all of the significant new models of 1950 had underfloor engines, though. There was the Bedford SB, forward control successor to the highly-successful normal control OB, and destined for a long and fruitful life; and there was the Foden PVR6, which completely defied convention with its transversely rear-mounted engine. Two engines were offered, the Gardner 6LW and Foden's own unusual two-stroke unit. The Foden anticipated fashion by at least ten years, but made no noticeable impact on the market; nor did another rear-engined model of the 1950s, the Rutland Clipper, which was built in small numbers in Surrey from 1956.

All the new chassis gave body designers much more scope and the coachbuilders had a brief, but extravagant, field day. The combination of increased dimensions and plain, flat fronts prompted some amazing confections; too often the designs attempted

the extreme front right from its conception, but there were operators who still preferred centre and even rear entrances, and some who fitted two doors, to improve passenger circulation. Another fad of the time was the standee single-decker, with a relatively low seating capacity, and extra room for standing passengers — a successful Continental idea which never really caught on in Britain. Most operators were glad of the extra seating capacity permitted by the new chassis. Normally, up to 44-45 seated passengers could be carried, a decided improvement on the 35/39 passengers in the equivalent front-engined models.

Successful as many of the early underfloor buses undoubtedly were, the growing need for economy prompted a widespread movement in favour of lighter-weight buses. At times in the 1950s this almost became an obsession, but towards the end of the decade reason gradually returned. This desire for more economical chassis spawned a new breed of chassis, spearheaded by Leyland's Tiger Cub and AEC's Reliance in 1952/53. In place of the 9.8/9.6litre engine of their heavyweight brothers, the Tiger Cub and Reliance offered considerably smaller engines. The 5.86litre 0350 engine was standard in the Tiger Cub, while the 7.68litre AV470 was the larger and more popular of the two Reliance engine options.

There soon followed lighter chassis like the Atkinson Alpha, Dennis Pelican and Guy Arab LUF, although some builders stuck to heavyweights. Daimler never ventured into the lightweight single-deck market. Their underfloor chassis, the Freeline, was introduced in 1951, but never sold in vast numbers, though Daimler's success in the double-deck market probably compensated for this.

The AEC Reliance and Leyland Tiger Cub easily dominated the field. Municipalities, independents and company fleets in the BET and Scottish Groups all took large deliveries of both chassis for coach and bus work. They both enjoyed long lives, too; the Tiger Cub lasted on the market until 1970 and the Reliance managed to pass the 20-year mark, rare for a British psv chassis, with a reduced, though continuing, demand.

Leeds was another city which abandoned its trams in the 1950s, and the replacement buses included this handsome 1959 Leyland Titan PD3/5 with 71-seat Roe body, seen here alongside an ex-London Feltham tramcar of 1930 vintage.

Walsall Corporation obtained special permission to operate these 30ft long trolleybuses in 1954, two years before the length was generally permitted for two-axle double-deckers. The first of the 22 Sunbeam F4As with 70-seat Willowbrook bodies is seen at Earls Court at the 1954 Commercial Show.

to disguise the essentially box-like shape of the underfloor-engined single-decker, and a mass of chrome and other brightwork was equated with passenger appeal, but slowly the designers learned the lesson that a subtle and straight-forward approach was the answer.

Coaches in the early 1950s usually had centre entrances, between the axles, but there were operators who continued to specify rear entrances. Gradually the bodybuilders perfected the fitment of one-piece coach doors ahead of the front axle and this layout increased in popularity. The underfloor-engined single-deck bus had an entrance at

Integral advantages

With notable exceptions, British busmen have been traditionally shy of the advantages of integral construction — until more recent times, at least. The integral bus, a complete structure without a separate chassis, had long been popular on the continent, and most private cars built during the last few decades have been integral. From a safety viewpoint,

integral construction produces a stronger vehicle, while there are also advantages in weight-saving. The early 1950s saw a veritable spate of new integral single-deckers. There were fairly successful vehicles like the AEC-Park Royal Monocoach, based on the Reliance chassis, and the Leyland-MCW Olympian, based on the Tiger Cub; they attracted at least a small number of faithful customers. Then there were the models which never really caught on, like the solitary Saro, the various Beadle-Commer types and the Harrington Contender, which at one stage in its career featured a Rolls-Royce petrol engine.

The one integral model which sold well was the Bristol-ECW LS, supplied only to the nationalised Tilling and Scottish fleets. It was, strictly speaking, semi-integral, as Bristol built the running units into an underframe which was capable of being driven to ECW Lowestoft for bodywork — and even, in a few cases, to Alexander at Stirling. Over 1,400 LSs, in both bus and coach form, were supplied between 1953 and 1957. Bristol's own AVW engine was available in the LS, as were the Gardner 5HLW and 6HLW units. The successor to the LS was the MW, introduced in 1957 and, interestingly, a separate chassis. In its ten-year life over 1,600 were built, again purely for nationalised fleets.

Midland Red had a head-start with the underfloor-engined single-decker; by 1950 it had around 400 in service and they had 25 million miles under their belts. Successive home-built BMMO models introduced further improvements and an interesting prototype appeared in 1953, featuring integral construction, rubber suspension, disc brakes and a fully-automatic gearbox; several of its revolutionary features appeared on the production S14 model which followed it, although the S14 had a conventional constant mesh gearbox.

Smaller and simpler buses were still required by many operators and the manufacturers tackled the problem of providing them in different ways. Bristol and ECW combined to produce the SC for BTC fleets, though only Tilling companies bought any. This simply-designed integral vehicle featured a front-mounted Gardner 4LK 3.8litre engine and a 35-seat bus body. In its six-year lifespan only slightly over 300 SCs were built, mainly for the Lincolnshire, Eastern Counties and Crosville fleets.

Albion offered a different solution, with its short-length underfloor Nimbus chassis, a rugged little bus which had only a limited success. The underfloor Albion engine also appeared in the Bristol SC's successor, the SU, introduced in 1960.

From this angle there is little clue that this 1952 Foden coach had a rear-mounted engine. It had a solid-looking 41-seat centre-entrance ACB body.

The full-size lightweight chassis market was really the province of Bedford's SB. First introduced in 1950 with a front-mounted petrol engine, the SB grew to a full 30ft model in 1955; in 1953 the Perkins R6 diesel engine was offered as an alternative and Bedford's own 300 engine appeared in 1959. The SB, often as not with coach bodywork by Duple, Plaxton or Burlingham, was the mainstay of many small coach fleets in the 1950s, when literally thousands were built.

The SB's main competitor in the early 1950s was the Commer Avenger, a chassis which had first appeared in 1949. It was unusual with its front-mounted underfloor petrol engine, but otherwise carried bodies similar to those fitted to Bedfords. In 1954 the Avenger was fitted with Commer's unusual TS3 (two-stroke, three-cylinder) diesel engine and in this guise continued in production for some years. The arrival of a new model from Ford in 1957, the Thames Trader coach chassis, largely narrowed the choice to Bedford and Ford.

The trend towards weight-saving and fuel economy had left a serious gap in the model lists — there was nothing really suitable for AEC and Leyland customers looking for a big-engined single-decker; the Regal and Royal Tiger underfloor models were by the mid-1950s aimed mainly at export customers. Leyland introduced a further export model in 1954, the Royal Tiger Worldmaster with the new 11.1litre 680 engine and a semi-automatic pneumocyclic gearbox. From 1956 a few of these were supplied to British customers, but in 1959 Leyland unveiled a new big-engined underfloor chassis, the Leopard, which

The Tiger Cub was Leyland's lightweight underfloor-engined model, and this 1952 prototype, with Saunders-Roe 44-seat body, is shown in trial service with Ribble in Lancashire. Its kerbside weight was kept under six tons.

combined the lighter chassis structure of the Tiger Cub with the 9.8litre 0600 engine of the Royal Tiger range. The new Leopard was an instant success, but the story of its success really belongs to the next chapter.

AEC answered the call for a larger engine with the new 9.6litre AV590 engine, offered in the Reliance as an alternative to the 7.68litre AV470.

Suiting London's needs

London Transport took delivery of two very different single-deck models in the 1950s. The AEC Regal had been a popular model with LT for many years and it was logical that the underfloor Regal IV should continue the tradition. London's first Regal IVs, classified RF, appeared in 1951, and over the next two years 700 were delivered. The first 25 RFs were 27ft 6in x 7ft 6in private hire coaches, while the remainder, admittedly 30ft long, were only 7ft 6in wide. There were also 15 8ft-wide Regal IVs built for London Transport, the ECW-bodied RFW class coaches.

But the most significant RFs were the 700 Metro-Cammell bodied vehicles, delivered initially as 25 private hire coaches, 263 Green Line coaches, 225 Central Area (red) buses and 187 Country Area (green) buses.

Other Regal IVs in London were the 65 attractive BEA airport coaches built for the services between Central London and the expanding Heathrow Airport. They followed an earlier tradition of deck-and-a-half coaches, with half the passengers in a raised rear portion, above a large luggage compartment. The Park Royal-bodied Regal IVs for BEA brought the roof line of the rear compartment forward at the same level.

London Transport experimented with demonstration vehicles from the manufacturers during the 1950s and at various times tried an AEC Monocoach, Bristol LS and Leyland Tiger Cub. Three AEC Reliances with Willowbrook bodies, class RW, were bought in 1960, but were short-lived. The only other single-deckers bought at the time were replacements for the ageing Leyland Cubs on the lighter-loading Country routes. There was no proprietary chassis which suited LT's needs, so a special version of the normal-control Guy Vixen was bought and fitted with 26-seat bodywork by Eastern Coach Works. There were 84 of these 25ft-long buses, fitted with Perkins P6 diesel engines, and they proved useful machines on one-man rural routes.

Throughout the world, though, the double-decker is synonymous with London and LT was still receiving large batches of RT variants in the early 1950s. The massive intake of new buses in the first postwar decade gave LT a really modern fleet, and their vehicle designers a chance to catch their breath and consider the London bus of the next decade. For a start, trolleybus replacement was in the offing, following the final tramway withdrawal in 1952, so a new double-deck design had to provide something like the 70 seats in LT's 30ft trolleybuses. Two-axle motor buses were still restricted to the 27ft length, but some coachbuilders were already managing to squeeze up to 66 passengers within the box dimensions of the time. The Routemaster, "London's Bus of the Future," was unveiled in 1954, a chassisless vehicle with the AEC 9.6litre engine and a 64-seat light alloy body; the whole bus weighed 6¾ tons — considerably

Tilling group purchases in the 1950s are well represented in this 1957 view inside the paint shop at Eastern National's central workshops at Chelmsford. They are all Bristol/ECW products — a 1957 60-seat Lodekka LD5G, a 1955 39-seat LS6B coach, and a 1954 LS5G 45-seat bus.

less than an RT. The prototype, RM1, had an LT-built sub-frame, fitted with fully-automatic transmission and featured independent front suspension and rear coil springs. Other prototype Routemasters followed, RM2 initially with a smaller engine for Country work, RM3 with Leyland engine and Weymann body, and CRL4 a coach version with Leyland engine and ECW body.

Four years after RM1's debut, the first production Routemaster was introduced incorporating many improvements and alterations, like power-assisted steering and warm-air heating. Although there had been a dramatic new development in double-deck bus design in the Routemaster's long gestation period, the compact, manoeuvrable and nippy RM, with its open rear platform, was the ideal bus for work in Central London.

If London Transport seemed to pursue rather individual policies, it was simply because it was so different from any other British transport undertaking. The sheer immensity of the LT area, and the vast fleet needed to serve it, put it in a very special position. At the end of 1953, for instance, the LT fleet of over 10,000 vehicles comprised 7,201 double-deckers, 893 single-deck buses, 372 coaches and 1,797 trolleybuses. The huge London fleet was particularly valuable when crowds of visitors thronged the

Metropolis for the Festival of Britain in 1951 and the Coronation in 1953.

Central London's unique traffic problems required unique solutions. Britain's first parking meters appeared on London streets in 1958 in an attempt to control the stream of private transport which seemed in danger of swamping the city. One of London Transport's solutions was BESI, the Bus Electronic Scanning Indicator, which allowed staff at a central control point to pinpoint individual buses on a small selection of routes, and to deal with abnormal service intervals and potential traffic jams.

If BESI was a sign of the times, so were bus strikes. The six-week strike by London Transport crews in the summer of 1958 was just another step in the steady erosion. Already, between 1950 and 1955, there had been a 10 per cent drop in passenger figures. An interesting side-effect of the 1958 strike was the reappearance of "pirates"; an odd assortment of buses appeared on some London streets, firstly illegally, but eventually with a certain amount of official blessing.

Dramatic changes

The design of the double-decker underwent dramatic changes in the 1950s. The Bristol/ECW Lodekka went into production in 1953 and sold in large numbers to Tilling and

Scottish fleets. The production Lodekka had a dropped centre double-reduction rear axle to keep the overall height down to 13ft 5in and was offered with Gardner 5LW or 6LW, or Bristol AVW engines. As regulations and requirements changed, so the Lodekka changed. After the change in dimensions in 1956 which permitted two-axle 30ft long double-deckers, Bristol built six prototypes to the new length and in 1958 a new flat-floor version appeared. From 1960 the flat-floor Lodekka became standard, offering 27ft or 30ft rear or forward entrance models. There were fresh engine options too when the Bristol BVW and Gardner 6LX units became available.

Bristol continued to build its tradtional K range in diminishing numbers for Tilling fleets until 1957. Improved, widened and lengthened versions of other well-proved double-deck chassis continued in production, but gradually the slower-selling chassis like the Albion Venturer, Crossley DD42, Dennis Lance and Foden PVD6 disppeared from the lists.

The main competition in the first half of the decade was between AEC's Regent and Leyland's Titan, particularly for the lucrative municipal tram-replacement business. AEC and Leyland were also favoured by the BET company fleets, but the main market for the Daimler CV and Guy Arab models was among the municipalities.

The so-called 'new-look' tin fronts which Midland Red and Foden had pioneered were adopted by the main builders. Daimler, Dennis and Guy used a style that had first appeared on Birmingham buses; Leyland adopted a design developed for Midland Red, while AEC at least chose a front-end structure that bore some resemblance to its distinctive traditional exposed radiator.

Cutting down weight and increasing passenger capacity became the preoccupations of the early 1950s, all in the interests of supposed economy. Double-deckers seating 66 passengers were not uncommon and it was often possible to reduce unladen weight to little over 6½tons, at a time when 7½-8tons was more normal. The chassis makers built better and lighter variations of their existing models and some operators favoured smaller engines as a possible aid to economy. The bigger engine usually won the day; as buses have become larger the power/weight ratio has become more important.

Most manufacturers gave double-deck operators the choice. Bristol, Daimler and Guy, for example, all offered either the 7litre Gardner 5LW or 8.4litre 6LW units. AEC offered a choice, too, between its 7.7litre and 9.6litre engines, but Leyland stuck to the one engine, the 9.8litre 0600. It was surprising, then, when a revolutionary new Leyland double-decker appeared in 1954, fitted with the 5.76litre 0350 unit — admittedly turbocharged. What was even more surprising was the position of the engine, as it was transversely mounted on the rear platform. This prototype, the Low-Loader, was used by several operators, and the data assembled was incorporated in the first Leyland Atlantean, which appeared in 1956.

The year 1956 was an important one for the double-decker. Two-axle 30ft deckers were at last legalised and most builders announced lengthened versions of their existing 27ft models. In addition to longer Regent Vs, AEC introduced the Bridgemaster, an integral low-floor model with Park Royal body, and Dennis announced the Loline, a version of the popular Bristol Lodekka built under licence and therefore available to non-nationalised firms.

Midland Red, of course, went its own way. Its main double-deck model in the early 1950s was the D7, a fairly orthodox vehicle with the BMMO 8litre engine and a constant mesh gearbox. Its 30ft successor appeared in 1958, the integral D9, with BMMO's 10.5litre engine, a semi-automatic gearbox, disc front brakes and rubber suspension. The 72-seat body had a traditional rear entrance, although many operators were turning towards forward entrances, behind the front axle; Midland Red had, in fact, featured a forward entrance on its immediate prewar

The Tilling group's medium capacity single-deck model in the 1950s was the Bristol/ECW SC, powered by the 3.8 litre Gardner 4LK engine. This 1956 Eastern Counties example is seen on a local route in Peterborough.

FEDD model and there had been a brief interest in this layout in the late 1930s. The arrival of the 30ft double-decker prompted a revival of the forward entrance, though the designs were often clumsy and often restricted passenger space.

Previous experience may have discouraged Midland Red from building front-engined forward entrance double-deckers in the 1950s, but the company was still looking to the future. While Leyland and Daimler were developing their rear-engined models, Midland Red was trying to adapt the underfloor layout for double-deckers. AEC had dabbled with an experimental underfloor chassis, but the essentially high floor level was always a problem. The two Midland Red D10 models which were built in 1960/61 overcame many of the problems, and was an advanced design with many of the features of the D9. In the event, Midland Red opted for a proprietary chassis, the Daimler Fleetline, as a successor to the D9 and no more home-made double-deckers were built.

But pride of place must go to the Atlantean, introducing a style of bus that is still very familiar today. The set-back front axle allowed an entrance alongside the driver and the engine — the big 0600 unit after all — was mounted transversely across the rear. The prototype Atlantean was integrally-built, a layout that was soon abandoned in favour of a separate chassis, but it was recognisably the forerunner of the standard double-decker of today, with its flat-fronted Metro-Cammell 78-seat body.

Production Atlantean chassis appeared in 1958 and Daimler followed with its Fleetline in 1960, initially with a Daimler CD6 engine, but the Gardner 6LX soon became standard. Gardner engines had been favourites with British bus operators since the first diesel engines appeared, and the addition of the 10.45litre 6LX in 1958 widened their appeal.

The 6LX engine was fitted in a last-ditch stand on behalf of the front-engined double-decker, the Wulfrunian, which helped bankrupt Guy and did very little else in the process. This revolutionary chassis first appeared in 1959, permitting bodies with the entrance ahead of the front axle and the staircase over the nearside front wheel. It featured air suspension and disc brakes, and the 6LX engine was sandwiched between the driver and the front platform. As a design it seemed sound — spoilt perhaps by operators' reluctance to accept this degree of sophistication. It was a spectacular failure and only 137 were built.

Transmission systems also advanced during the 1950s. The traditional friction clutch and constant mesh gearbox was favoured by Bristol, Dennis and Guy

customers, while Daimler stuck to its fluid flywheel/preselective gearbox, and Leyland offered a synchromesh gearbox. AEC offered both preselector and synchromesh boxes, but in the middle of the decade development of semi-automatic and fully-automatic epicyclic gearboxes was sufficiently advanced to persuade some of the major manufacturers to offer them as options. Normally the semi-automatic box was favoured, permitting direct gear selection without the need for a clutch pedal, but some operators, notably London Transport, specified fully-automatic boxes. The rear-engined double-deck Atlantean and

Top: **The London Transport GS class, Guy Vixens with ECW 26-seat bodies, was first introduced in 1953 for lightly-loaded country routes such as this one in the Watford area.** *Above:* **The Routemaster was London Transport's standard double-deck purchase from 1959 to 1965. This is a standard short-length RM, one of the first delivered, at Hammersmith in 1971.**

Fleetline models were only available with the new epicyclic transmission systems.

Daimler, with over 20 years' experience of preselectors, introduced an alternative synchromesh gearbox in 1958 and five years later replaced this with a Guy constant-mesh box.

Motorways and Hostesses

If the 1950s saw the start of the slow decline in passenger figures and the start of the fare rise spiral, it also saw steady improvement on the coaching side. Bigger and (sometimes) better coaches gave operators an incentive to develop new long-distance and express services. In Scotland, for instance, Northern Roadways obtained licences to operate from Edinburgh and Glasgow to London, traditionally the territory of Scottish Omnibuses and Western SMT. The fare for the Northern Roadways overnight 'Pullman De Luxe Sleeper Night Coach' was £2, when the established operators still charged 30s (£1.50), but Northern Roadways offered hostesses and snacks. The Northern Roadways venture was comparatively short-lived, but their competition at least prompted the Scottish Group fleets to re-equip their services with coaches which featured reclining seats, individual reading lights and toilet accommodation.

The competition between coach operators of all sizes was emphasised in 1955 when the first British Coach Rally was held at Clacton, an opportunity for friendly rivalry between firms, and a chance for the general public to see an impressive array of hardware.

Coach design took an important step forward when Plaxton announced the Panorama body in 1958. Its main features were the unusually long side windows, which were of obvious benefit to coach operators and which started a fashion that caught on very quickly.

The opening of the Preston bypass in 1958 was another significant event in the development of coach travel, for this was Britain's first stretch of motorway. The next year 73 miles of the M1 motorway were opened and coach operators throughout the country were quick to realise its potential. In November 1959, Midland Red introduced a Birmingham-London motorway service which cut nearly two hours from the established coach service timings; at one stage it was responsible for a staggering 900 per cent increase in through passengers between the two cities. The fast timings and the low fares won the day, for the coach fare

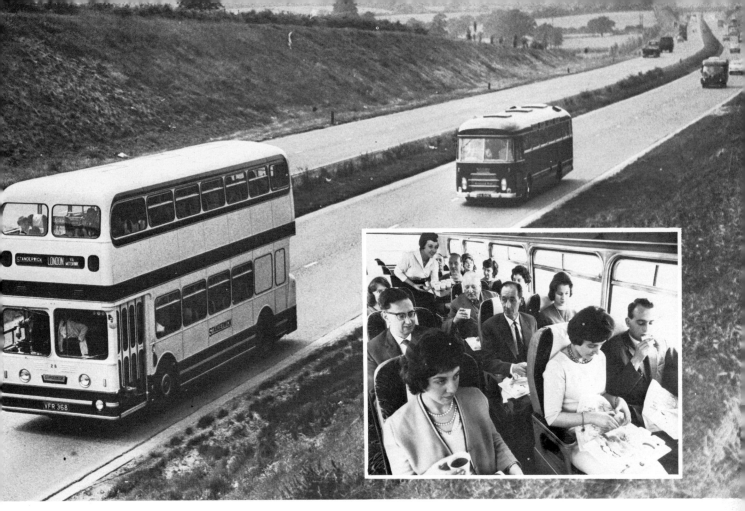

of 21s 3d (£1.06) compared well with the rail fare of 42s (£2.10). The coaches used on the Midland Red services were BMMO-built CM5Ts, capable of sustained 80mph running.

Ribble had different ideas about motorway coaches; its Gay Hostess coaches were *double*-deckers. The double-deck coach has never been really successful in Britain; even in the 1920s there were double-deck coaches, but then and subsequently the idea never became widespread. Ribble had always supported this layout and in the late 1940s had introduced its famous White Ladies, Leyland Titan coaches. The Gay Hostesses were something rather different and were not simply double-deck buses with fancy trimmings and coach seats.

They were Leyland Atlanteans, then a fairly new model, with MCW bodies seating 50 (34/16), and featured an impressive list of coach features; there were reclining seats, individual reading lights, parcel racks and toilet and kitchen accommodation. Ribble and subsidiary Standerwick were justly proud of these impressive vehicles and introduced the prototype in 1959 in a characteristic blaze of glory. In a booklet welcoming passengers aboard 'this fabulous and luxurious vehicle' Ribble enthused: 'May we tell you what is our aim in providing a magnificent vehicle of the kind in which you are now riding? It is to give you, the

passenger, greater comfort and added amenities at our current low fares'.

The Gay Hostess carried a steward or hostess who sold light refreshments during the journey and who 'will be pleased to help you in every way possible and at intervals will make announcements of interest over the excellent public address system'. The Gay Hostess prototype was joined by a fleet of production coaches and by some less-luxurious versions, the second generation of White Ladies, but the Ribble Group was the only big operator to support double-deck coaches.

Among the manufacturers there was little activity. Leyland acquired Albion, the long-established Scottish bus and truck builder, in 1951, an early stage in its empire-building that was to gain momentum in the 1960s. One possible liaison that never materialised was a proposed merger between Leyland and Rolls-Royce in 1959, but Leyland was more interested in arch-enemy AEC, which was suffering at the time from its price-cutting war with Leyland. Leyland and AEC were to remain defiantly independent for a few more years, but one merger which anticipated the dramatic changes of the next decade was Jaguar's acquisition of Daimler, in 1960. And the next decade was certainly to prove one of the most significant in the story of the motor bus.

Ribble and Midland Red both developed special coaches for use on motorway services. This 1965 view on the Meriden Bypass shows a Gay Hostess from the fleet of Ribble subsidiary Standerwick; these were Leyland Atlanteans with 50-seat MCW coach bodies. Midland Red built it own coaches for motorway use, like the 1965 CM6T at the rear. Inside the Gay Hostesses (*inset*) passengers received a wide selection of meals.

THE
DUPLE
COACH

Enclosed full-size coaches have seen some amazing design advances since the early 1930s when they really came into their own. The products of Duple, for long one of Britain's leading coachbuilders, illustrate some of the changes.

The 1930 AEC Regal in the first photo, part of the original Green Line fleet, shows the bus-like lines of many early coaches, but by 1933 distinctive styles were developing, as on this Regal for John Bull (Wood, Blackpool), which featured toilet accommodation and a roof luggage rack. The third photo shows another AEC Regal, a 1939 example for Northern General, with subtly streamlined styling for touring work. The roof luggage compartment is still there, but designed to match the lines of the coach.

The 1946 Regal for Cotter's, Glasgow, has obvious roots in the 1939 body, this was the famous A type, a popular and much-imitated classic.

Duple produced several coach styles for the early underfloor-engined chassis, and the Elizabethan design of 1953, seen here on AEC Reliance chassis, was one of the more successul. For the lighter-weight front-engined chassis there was the Vega range of bodies, shown on Bedford SB chassis for Davis, Sevenoaks.

The Bella Vega range marked a return to squarer body styles, and featured one-piece windscreens and an unusual rear-end treatment, here on 1964 Bedford SB chassis for Buckmaster, Leighton Buzzard. This was superseded by the crisply-styled Viceroy range, seen here on 1970 Bedford YRQ mid-engined chassis.

The current Duple range centres round the Dominant, first introduced in 1972. This 1973 example, on Bedford YRT chassis, is in National white livery for the Shamrock & Rambler fleet. The Dominant 2 was added to the range in 1976, featuring a deeper windscreen and revised front and rear styling, and is shown here on AEC Reliance chassis for Smiths Happiway-Spencers.

The AEC Swift was just one of the 1960s rash of rear-engined models. This Willowbrook-bodied demonstrator is seen on a test run in 1965.

The Sting in the Tail

1961-1968

The 1960s were unsettled years for the bus business. There were changes in all sectors of the industry, but the major changes came after much-needed new legislation altered the whole face of road passenger transport in Britain; the far-reaching effects of the 1968 Transport Act will be considered in the final chapter.

In the early 1960s the continuing decline in passengers and the continuing lack of suitable staff forced the bus industry to take a long hard look at itself. While some operators adopted a defeatist attitude, dismissing these factors as inevitable, others set out to salvage the healthy part of their operations and took steps to stop the rot that was setting in to the rest. Many saw one-man operation as an answer and set about converting existing vehicles; sometimes this was enough to give the kiss-of-life to ailing rural routes, but often it had been left too late.

One-man operation has always been around, but many large operators shied clear of it until it was almost too late. Some urban fleets tried ambitious schemes on a fairly large scale; Sunderland Corporation designed two-door single-deckers to accept special pre-purchased tokens, but the scheme was a failure. London Transport, as we shall see, also placed its faith in two-door single-deckers with sophisticated equipment and these enjoyed a relative degree of success. But even one-man operation failed to save many services and time and time again operators found it quite impossible to retain some routes. In some cases independent operators stepped in to keep services going, but some only confirmed the findings of their bigger brothers.

After a long fight, one-man *double*-deckers were legalised from July 1966, a change which was to have far-reaching effects, particularly in urban fleets. After a few tentative experiments at places like Brighton and Great Yarmouth, one-man double-deckers were soon appearing throughout Britain, helping to alleviate some of the more serious staffing problems.

Another important consequence of this development was its effect on double-deck bus design. The traditional double-decker of the 1950s, a front-engined 27-footer with open rear platform, was still in favour, as was its 30ft counterpart. Many 30-footers, but fewer 27-footers, were being built with forward entrances behind the front axle. Challenging these, Leyland's rear-engined Atlantean was selling steadily, to be joined by Daimler's Fleetline when production got under way in 1962. But the front-engined designs still had life in them and new models were still appearing, though the manufacturers were concentrating on the low-floor chassis which only Bristol, with its restricted Lodekka model, had successfully explored. Leyland's attempt was the Lowlander, a low-floor model based on the Titan, but built at the Albion plant in Glasgow. Its main support came from fleets in the Scottish Bus Group, where it succeeded late-model lowbridge Titans — possibly the last large-scale stronghold of the old side-gangway layout. Dennis introduced the Mark III version of its Loline model in 1961, featuring a different clutch and constant mesh gearbox, and it was built fitfully for a few more years. The integral AEC/Park Royal Bridgemaster was phased out in 1963 after a none-too-successful life; its replacement, the

Forward-entrance double-deckers became popular in the late 1950s/early 1960s. This Bradford Corporation AEC Regent V was new in 1959 with MCW 70-seat coachwork.

Renown, first appeared in 1962, a low-floor model available as a separate chassis. Its suspension layout was more conventional than that on the Bridgemaster and a semi-automatic gearbox was offered as an option. Guy had a stab at this market with the Arab V, first built in 1962, but this was not a true low-height model, permitting bodies to be built to the height of around 14ft, between the 'lowbridge' and 'highbridge' heights.

None of these models really caught on, though much of this reluctance was due to the alternatives offered by the new rear-engined models. Here was the basis for a modern-looking bus, with seats for up to 78 passengers, and the dropped-centre rear axle of the Daimler Fleetline permitted 13ft 6in high double-deckers with normal seating on both decks; the early low-height Atlantean PDR1/1s needed a semi-lowbridge side-gangway upper deck. Although a true low-height Atlantean, the PDR1/2, appeared in 1964, it never achieved the success of the Fleetline. Once production of the Fleetline really got into full swing, the movement towards rear-engined buses really gained momentum. Municipalities, BET company fleets and even independents all bought Atlanteans or Fleetlines — sometimes both — with amazingly uninspired bodies by the main coachbuilders. Gradually, often at the instigation of the operator, more attractive body designs appeared; notable among these were the styles supplied to municipalities like Bolton, Glasgow, Liverpool, Manchester, Nottingham, Oldham and Sheffield.

Not every operator went overboard for rear-engined buses. The Tilling Group stuck to the well tried Bristol/ECW Lodekka as its double-deck model, and the 70-seat forward-entrance FLF variant was supplied in increasing numbers; there was even a 31ft model with seats for up to 78 passengers. The Scottish Bus Group bought both Lodekkas and Albion Lowlanders for several years, but moved on to Daimler Fleetlines in due course. Some municipal operators stuck faithfully to the traditional 27ft rear open platform double-decker, though as things turned out they were not to have a lot of choice in the matter.

Various changes in the manufacturing industry hastened the demise of the front-engined double-decker. Jaguar Cars, which had bought over Daimler in 1960, rescued the ailing Guy business the following year, bringing two old rivals under the same management. Two even deadlier rivals came together in 1962 when Leyland bought out AEC, joining Standard-Triumph in what was to become the Leyland Motor Corporation. A share exchange with Bristol gave Leyland another useful foothold, and brought Bristol chassis and ECW bodies on to the open market for the first time in 17 years. The Leyland empire-building continued in 1966 when Rover was acquired — the same year that Jaguar's parallel expansion had brought about a merger with the British Motor Corporation to produce British Motor Holdings. The biggest merger of all, between Leyland and BMH, was very much on the cards from this time, but in the end Leyland took over the sickly BMH in 1968 to form the British Leyland Motor Corporation. Under the British Leyland umbrella on the bus side were chassis-makers AEC, Albion, Daimler, Guy and Leyland, and body-builders Park Royal and Roe, plus the interests in Bristol and ECW.

Two low-height double-deckers of the 1960s. *Below left:* **The Albion Lowlander, a relatively unsuccessful model, represented by this Northern Counties 71-seater in the fleet of the independent South Notts company; Lowlanders sold outside Scotland carried the 'Leyland' name.** *Below:* **The most successful of the low-height models — the Bristol/ECW Lodekka, here in 30ft forward-entrance FLF form, in Bristol in 1969.**

The old order and the new at Leeds. The traditional front-engined/rear entrance double-decker — a 1962 Roe-bodied AEC Regent V — and its rear engined/front entrance successor — a 1967 Roe-bodied Daimler Fleetline, both from the Leeds City Transport fleet.

All of these changes affected the bus chassis built by the manufacturers involved. The long-running AEC Regent, Bristol Lodekka, Daimler CV, Guy Arab and Leyland Titan models were all gradually phased out by the end of the 1960s, leaving the rear-engined Atlantean and Fleetline models to meet the demand for double-deckers. They were, however, joined by a third model, the Bristol VRL, which was first introduced in 1966. The VRL was another rear-engined design, but featured a Gardner 6LX engine mounted longtitudinally in the rear offside corner, rather than the more common transverse layout. The prototype VRLs were 33ft long and were among the first double-deckers to take real advantage of the 1961 change in dimensions which permitted psvs of up to 36ft x 8ft 2½in. Double-deckers of around 31ft were found in many areas, but Daimler and Leyland only introduced 33ft versions of their Fleetline and Atlantean models in 1966. Several operators were quick to specify the longer chassis, sometimes with up to 86 seats, but many reverted to the more manageable 31-footers. To cater for the longer chassis and for a widespread demand for more powerful buses, bigger engines became available in 1966; Gardner's beefier 6LXB was soon appearing in Daimler Fleetlines; Leyland introduced the 11.1litre 680 engine as an alternative to the popular 9.8litre 600; AEC replaced the AV590 unit in the Regent V with the 11.3litre AV691.

A transverse-engined version of the Bristol VR, designated VRT, appeared in 1967, and few VRLs have been built. The VRT became the standard Tilling Group double-decker and the Lodekka was no longer listed,

although the model did feature in the 1968 Tilling bus order. The early VRT was not a complete success, suffering perhaps from a rush to get it into service — not for the VRT the old Tilling tradition of building a handful of prototypes for extensive proving trials before production started. A most unusual version of the longtitudinal-engined VRL appeared at the 1968 Commercial Motor Show, a 36ft 60-seat double-deck coach for Standerwick. The Leyland 680 engine shared the rear portion of the lower deck with toilet and luggage accommodation, for only 18 of the seats were downstairs. Another 36ft double-decker was on show at Earls Court in 1968 and it too had a longtitudinal rear engine. It was a Daimler CR36, for Walsall Corporation, with an offside-mounted Cummins engine and an 86-seat Northern Counties body. The engine position allowed a doorway to be fitted behind the rear axle and there was also a door in the more traditional front position. Two staircases were fitted, for the entrance was at the front, with stairs behind the driver, and the rear stairs were over the engine, leading to the rear exit — and supervised by a television camera. Neither of these 36ft designs was really successful. The Standerwick Bristol VRL was joined by a production batch and they did some useful work on motorway services; but the Walsall Daimler was to remain unique and had a short life for such an advanced and expensive design.

With the arrival of one-man double-deckers, the final death-knell of the familiar front-engined designs was really sounding, and by the end of the 1960s the last examples of the AEC Regent, Daimler CV and Leyland Titan had been delivered. In their

place, operators were taking increasing numbers of two-door double-deckers, with a front-entrance for one-man operation and a central exit, usually immediately behind the front axle. Some really crisp designs were coming from British coachworks, like the classically simple standard design from Park Royal and the trend-setting Mancunian style for Manchester Corporation. These marked a final break from the long-running designs which many builders insisted on producing, and which made no allowance for the totally different lines of the rear-engined double-decker.

Longer single-deckers

While all this was going on in the double-deck market, the single-deck world was far from quiet. The immediate effects of the 1961 legislation which permitted 36ft buses were merely longer versions of AEC's Reliance and Leyland's Leopard, though by 1962 the manufacturers were beginning to catch their breath and a veritable rash of new designs appeared that year. There was Bedford's 36ft model, the VAL, with a front-mounted engine, but with an entrance at the extreme front, ahead of twin-steering axles, for the VAL was a six-wheeler, a unique solution to the length problem. Bristol's 36-footer was equally unconventional for the time, as the RE featured a horizontally-mounted rear engine; this was a layout that soon became familiar throughout Britain, but the RE was certainly the first — and possibly the best — of the 1960s rear-engined designs. Daimler showed an experimental rear-engined chassis at the 1962 Commercial Show, but it was two more years before a production version appeared.

The front engine retained a wide circle of admirers, particularly where front entrances could be offered. The Bedford VAL spearheaded the resurrection of interest, supported by the Thames 36, and less successful models from Albion and Dodge. The Thames 36, later called the Ford R1114 and eventually to become the R1114, was joined by a 32ft model in 1965, the Ford R192, later the R1014. Bedford's 32ft equivalent was the VAM and, with the six-wheel VAL and the two Ford models, represented the mainstay of many a coach operator in the 1960s.

Bristol's clear lead with the rear-engined RE chassis was followed up by several new models first seen in 1964. There were AEC's Swift and Merlin, Daimler's Roadliner and Leyland's Panther and Panther Cub.

The 36ft AEC Swift featured a horizontal AH505 8.2litre engine mounted at the rear of a low-frame or high-frame chassis. The low-frame Swift was intended for urban work, where an easier front entrance and interior floor height would be useful; the high-frame version, for tour and express work, permitted underfloor lockers in place of the normal rear luggage boot. Constant mesh and semi-automatic gearboxes were offered and a bigger engine, the 11.3litre AH691, was also offered, though in this form the chassis was strictly designated Merlin. A 33ft Swift was a further option. With the Swift, according to contemporary publicity, AEC put 'the sting in the tail'.

Leyland's Panther family was similar. Low-frame and high-frame versions of the 36ft Panther were introduced and the 9.8litre 600 engine was mounted horizontally, coupled to a semi-automatic pneumocyclic

Bedford adopted this unusual twin-steering front axle layout for its first 36ft model, the VAL. This example, with Duple Viceroy coach body, was new in 1968 to the Grey-Green fleet.

gearbox. The low-frame Panther Cub, with the 6.45litre 400 engine, was intended for buses around 33ft long.

Daimler tackled the rear-engined problem rather differently. Its Roadliner featured a vertically-mounted vee-form engine, the compact 9.63litre Cummins V6-200, and full air suspension as standard. Only a low-frame 36ft model was offered.

None of the new chassis was a complete success. A few were bought for coach work, but the majority were used for close-frequency urban work in a variety of centres. London Transport, as we shall see, bought a large fleet of Merlins and Swifts, but suffered from the same problems as its provincial brothers.

A different type of rear-engined chassis appeared in 1965 when Albion introduced its VK43L Viking model. The Viking name had reappeared in 1963 on the front-engined VK41L model, a 32ft lightweight chassis with a Leyland 400 engine mounted at the front; now the VK43 placed this engine vertically at the rear. The result was a fairly rugged lightweight chassis which proved successful with fleets in the Scottish Bus Group, although it was not widely bought outside Scotland. Other activity in the rear-engined market was Daimler's single-deck version of the Fleetline, following a batch of single-deck Fleetlines which were supplied in 1965 to Birmingham City Transport.

One of the more successful 1960s single-deckers was the Bristol LH, replacing the rare SU. With Bristols back on the open market, a lightweight underfloor-engined chassis was called for, available in various lengths up to 36ft. Two engines, the Leyland 400 and Perkins 6.354, were available, and

the LH proved a reliable and useful machine, both as a rural bus for Tilling fleets and as a coach model for nationalised and independent fleets.

In the single-deck bus field, the 1960s saw a much more positive move towards vehicle standardisation and by the middle of the decade several clearly-identified patterns were evolving. The independent busman buying a new bus would often as not choose a Bedford or Ford, with coachwork by Plaxton, Strachans or Willowbrook; some chose heavier chassis, like the AEC Reliance or Leyland Leopard, but still patronised the same coachbuilders. The Tilling fleets had the Bristol RELL, with attractive ECW body, while the Scottish Group favoured the Alexander Y-type body, on AEC Reliance, Bristol RE or Leyland Leopard for heavyweights, or Albion Viking and Bedford VAM for lightweights. The company fleets controlled by BET had a wider range of suppliers, though, as always, AECs and Leylands were predominant. A few bought Daimler's Roadliner, while the wider availability of Bristol's RE brought it into a number of fleets. Several builders were required to supply the needs of BET fleets, but a functional standardised design was evolved in the early 1960s, and built by a number of coachbuilders throughout the country. This neat design, with its wrap-round front and rear windscreens, was adopted by several builders as a standard single-deck style and guaranteed it a long life.

With fewer builders and fewer models, the luxury coach market lost much of its variety at this time. In the main, the independents stuck to Bedford and Ford for chassis, and Duple and Plaxton for bodies, though an increasing number bought Reliances and Leopards. Duple and Plaxton reigned supreme in the heavyweight coach market too, particularly when Harrington withdrew from the field in 1965.

Experiments in London

In London, where standardisation had always been essential, the 1960s were typified by the lack of it. The Routemaster was entering service in large numbers — number 1,000 was delivered in 1961, London's 21,669th AEC. But the design had been conceived some years before and had been overtaken by changes in fashion and regulation. A 30ft Routemaster was designed in 1961 by inserting a short extra bay into the standard RM shell and many of the later Routemasters were 30ft RMLs. A variation was RMF1254, a forward-entrance 30ft Routemaster, but although it was demonstrated to various operators in Britain this bus never entered LT service and was sold to Northern General, where it joined 50 similar vehicles which had been bought direct after the Routemaster went on to the open market. The only other Routemasters built were short forward-entrance vehicles supplied to BEA and ironically some of these were bought by London in 1975 to alleviate a vehicle shortage; the "problems" of operating RMF1254 were conveniently forgotten.

The adaptability of the basic Routemaster design was further illustrated when 68 RMCs 57-seat coaches with rear air suspension and platform doors were delivered in 1962 for the Green Line fleet. The last Routemasters, 30ft buses and coaches, were built in 1967/68, to bring the class to 2,760 vehicles. There was also a very advanced rear-engined bus, FRM1, which used more than 60 per cent RM parts, but in spite of its sophisticated specification and apparent potential — many regard it as one of the finest double-deckers built in recent years — the project was abandoned.

While the Routemaster family was satisfying immediate needs, LT was looking ahead to the next generation of London bus and ordered several batches of experimental vehicles. The first to enter service in 1965 were eight Daimler Fleetlines for the Country Area, followed by 50 Leyland Atlanteans for the Central Area and 14 AEC Reliance coaches for the Green Line fleet. The most significant of the new orders, though, were the six AEC Merlins with bodies seating 25 and with standing room for a further 48 passengers 'for experiments in handling big surges of rush-hour passengers in Central London, for example between main line termini and business centres'.

Above: **One of the first generation of London Transport Red Arrows, an AEC Merlin with Strachans body, which entered service in 1966 on service 500, the first of the network of fast, flat-fare urban services.** *Left:* **Inside a Red Arrow, showing the ticket machines, turnstiles, the large forward standing area, and the 25 seats at the rear.**

When these buses did enter service, in April 1966, they were the first of the famous Red Arrows and as such merit closer examination.

Boarding at the wide front entrance, passengers were confronted by two turnstiles, released only when a 6d (2½p) coin was placed in the slot. All 25 seats were in the rear portion of the bus, behind the central exit doors, while the front part of the bus was for standing passengers only. The first Red Arrow service was between Victoria Station and Marble Arch and operated only during the Monday-Friday 'working' hours of 07.30 and 19.15. The fast, flat-fare Red Arrows were very different from normal London concepts, but caught on quickly and were joined by a small network of similar services.

The Red Arrows were a glimpse of future

standing accommodation should be provided on shorter routes and that new methods of fare collection should be worked out. The ideas were good on paper, but time has shown that not all worked in practice.

The basic network of trunk routes, using two-man double-deckers, was to be supplemented by Red Arrow type buses in the West End and the City, and fed by suburban satellite routes operated by one-man single-deckers. 'Experience with the Red Arrow buses shows that a high proportion of standing accommodation is acceptable to short-distance passengers, who are the great majority on Central Area's buses', commented London Transport, and it seemed that LT had turned against the double-decker. Certainly, the high-capacity double-deckers favoured by other operators found little support in London, where the official feeling was that 'little more can be done to increase the effective capacity of the two-man double-decker. If the bus is so big that the conductor cannot get round it in time to collect all the fares, it is not efficient. In London, where many passengers ride for short distances only, the 72-seater is the largest vehicle of the present type that can be operated practically.'

In any case, large orders for AEC Merlin single-deckers were placed and in 1968/69 a total of 650 Merlins were bought — a mixture of Red Arrows and one-door and two-door buses, with different ratios of seated/standing passengers, for Central and Country routes. Many of the new Merlins entered service in September 1968, when a massive revision of LT services was undertaken, incorporating many of the proposals in the reshaping plan. There were seven new Red Arrow routes, and rail-linked suburban schemes at Walthamstow, connecting with the new underground Victoria Line, and at Wood Green. For a multitude of reasons, not all of these services were a complete success and the Merlins were never the happiest buses in London service. More rear-engined AECs were bought, but these were the shorter Swift model, generally a more successful design, and with the very last Routemaster double-deckers entering service in 1968, the next breed of London bus was to be very different to its predecessors.

Electrification, for and against

But London Transport was not the only transport undertaking with problems in the 1960s. Far from it. The same factors that were making life difficult in London were affecting transport fleets, large and small, throughout Britain. And it was not only road passenger transport that was suffering. British Railways incurred a loss of

trends, for a few months after they first appeared an important report, *Reshaping London's Bus Services*, was published detailing many of LT's forward plans. It was drawn up as a result of the continuing decline after passenger totals reached their peak in 1948 and the problems that followed. There were the growing difficulties of congestion caused by the private car, particularly acute in Central London, and the shortage of suitable staff to man the buses. To overcome these difficulties, LT plumped for radically different techniques. The plan proposed that routes should be shortened, that one-man operation should be extended, that more

£87million and clearly drastic action was required to prevent this situation worsening. One outcome was the Beeching Report of 1963, which proposed axing 5,000 miles of unprofitable lines, from the total route mileage of 17,000 miles. The effects of the Beeching cuts were drastic, but proved only to be a holding action in the face of a deteriorating economic situation. One bright spot on the railway horizon was the onward spread of electrification. In 1960 the first stage of the West Coast electrification was completed, from Crewe to Manchester, and in 1966 the section from London Euston to Crewe was finished, bringing dramatically improved journey times and a more reliable service.

While the railways regarded electrification as a solution for the future, municipal operators were abandoning electric traction as fast as they could. Glasgow, the last stronghold of real street tramways, fell in 1962, while the trolleybus conversions of the 1960s left only a handful of faithfuls at the end of the decade. London, Ipswich, Hull, Rotherham, Manchester, Newcastle, Nottingham, Derby, Glasgow, Maidstone and Belfast were just some of the fleets which went completely over to motor buses at the time. Britain's last new trolleybus was delivered in 1962 to Bournemouth Corporation, one of only a handful of survivors by 1968.

On an encouraging note, the efforts of the Tramway Museum Society were beginning to bear fruit. Formed in 1955 to establish a working tramway museum, the Society had bought a site in 1959, a disused quarry at Crich in Derbyshire, and by 1964 members of the public were able to relive the pleasures of electric tramcar rides. Since that time the Tramway Museum at Crich has grown to become a deservedly popular tourist attraction and houses an impressive collection of trams from British and overseas systems, ranging from 19th century examples through to trams built after World War II, which never had the chance to live their full lives on their parent tramways.

The bus preservation movement was making impressive advances, too. Only a few of the old buses had been set aside for preservation in the early days, some by private individuals, but most notably by London General/London Transport, which had saved examples of its most significant bus models, though for many years these were not on public exhibition. The conversion of LT's former Clapham depot to the Museum of British Transport gave the public the first opportunity of examining these priceless vehicles properly. The first portion of Clapham, with small exhibits only, opened

Top: **From the Museum of British Transport at Clapham, the 1920 ex-London General K type takes to the road for the 1966 London-Brighton historic commercial vehicle run. Compare it with the RT, thirty years its junior.** *Above:* **The later London Transport Routemasters were 30ft 72-seat RML models. One of these is seen in Staines after the LT Country Area had become the NBC-controlled London Country.** *Left:* **The unique London rear-engined Routemaster, FRM1, on a local service in the Croydon area. This advanced bus incorporated a large proportion of standard Routemaster parts.**

Albion's lightweight rear-engined Viking model was widely bought by the Scottish Bus Group. This Alexander (Midland) version at Oban in 1968 carries an Alexander Y-type body, a design that remained SBG's single-deck standard for many years.

Dissatisfaction with the products from leading coachbuilders led several operators to prepare striking new designs of their own. Manchester Corporation's Mancunian design of 1968 was a trend setter, and this is a Park Royal-bodied Daimler Fleetline 73-seater, on a one-man operated service; Manchester was an early user of one-man double-deckers on a large scale.

in 1961 and in 1963 the Museum proper was opened, with a fine collection of railway relics and sections devoted to buses, trams and trolleybuses, mainly the London Transport vehicles, augmented by various other museum-pieces acquired by the BTC. Another important collection was placed on show when the Glasgow Museum of Transport opened in 1964, using the Glasgow Corporation tramcar collection as the centrepiece, and containing many examples of Scottish-built cars and commercials, including a Glasgow Albion bus. A further section was later added, containing a number of Scottish railway locomotives.

Private preservation was becoming very popular at the same time and an increasing number of rallies was being organised to allow the proud owners to exhibit their vehicles. The first of the Historic Commercial Vehicle Club's famous Brighton Runs was held in 1962 and such events have multiplied many times since then, with scores of rallies each season, attended by some of

what must now be thousands of preserved buses and coaches.

While the preservationists were looking fondly backward, the bus industry was viewing the future with growing concern. If the problems of the 1960s were to be faced and overcome, changes would be necessary to the structure of the industry and to the legislation which controlled it. The first public intimation of the changes which were to follow was contained in a White Paper presented in 1966 and followed the next year by a more detailed document which contained several far-reaching proposals. A new Transport Act was promised and this would help establish a more efficient transport structure. In four important areas, Birmingham, Manchester, Liverpool and Newcastle, new conurbation authorities would be set up, using the existing municipal bus operators as a base. The Transport Holding Company bus interests in England and Wales would be replaced by a new body, the National Bus Company, which was to control not only the Tilling fleets, but also those of the rival BET Group, which, only months before the White Paper was published in 1967, had agreed to sell out to THC for £35 million.

The Scottish Bus Group was to pass into the control of a new body, the Scottish Transport Group, which would also take over the road and sea services of David MacBrayne and the railway-owned Caledonian Steam Packet shipping fleet.

At the same time it was announced that a major reorganisation of London Transport was also on the cards, for LT's Central Area operations were to pass into the direct control of the Greater London Council, and a new company, London Country Bus Services Ltd, would operate the Country Area and Green Line services under the control of the new National Bus Company.

Late in 1968 the Transport Act became law and in 1969 things really started to change.

Symbolic of the new thinking in the bus industry — a Leyland National on one of London Country's successful Superbus services in Stevenage.

Properly Integrated and Efficient

The Years from 1969

January 1, 1969 was an important day in the story of road passenger transport in Great Britain. On that date two new authorities assumed control of Britain's company buses — the Scottish Transport Group in Scotland, and the National Bus Company in England and Wales. The Scottish body was given wider-ranging powers, for the new STG controlled not only the Scottish Bus Group, but also the Caledonian Steam Packet company (the former British Railways shipping services on the Firth of Clyde), and the THC half-share in David MacBrayne Ltd, operating shipping, haulage and bus services in Scotland's western highlands and islands. The STG inherited 4,862 buses and a bus-operating staff of 18,125.

National Bus, with the rest of the THC fleets, brought the newly-merged Tilling and BET companies under common management, with a total fleet of 20,637 buses and a staff of 80,344.

The formation of STG and NBC were just two results of the 1968 Transport Act, comprehensive and far-reaching legislation which altered the whole structure of the bus industry. One of its best-known provisions, Section 34, allowed local authorities to make grants towards bus services where retention of a loss-making facility was considered essential. Section 34 was to affect the pattern of bus services provided in many rural areas.

Another grant which had important repercussions was the bus grant, which provided 25 per cent towards the cost of new buses that complied with a set of specifications designed to encourage the introduction of more up-to-date vehicles and the spread of one-man operation.

Grant-eligible single-deckers could be high-floor vehicles, in 9m, 10m or 11m lengths, or low-floor buses in 10m or 11m lengths. In effect this meant that most current models, whether front, underfloor or rear-engined, were eligible. Manual, semi-automatic or fully-automatic transmission could be fitted, as could either manual or power steering. It was assumed that high-floor models would be single-doored, although centre exit doors were optional on low-floor chassis.

For ease of passenger flow, acceptable floor heights and door widths were detailed, and a minimum power/weight ratio was laid down to ensure adequate performance.

The double-deck grant specifications were rather more restrictive, for only transverse rear-engined models were included, presumably on the basis that front-engined double-deckers were not normally suitable for one-manning. Normal-height double-deckers, in both 9.5m and 10m lengths, were

eligible for the grant, as were 9.5m low-height models. The most familiar variant, the 9.5m normal-height double-decker, could have one or two doors, semi or fully-automatic transmission, powered or manual steering; the 10m version had to have two doors, and powered steering. The low-height specification assumed only a single, front, door.

The bus grants were immediately welcomed as a means of re-equipping and standardising fleets, and a chance to expand one-man operation. The specifications were, in the main, well thought out, and covered the most familiar types of vehicle entering service in Britain at that time, allowing for local prejudices and preferences. There was room, too, for less orthodox vehicles to suit peculiar operating conditions and special approval could normally be obtained to secure a grant in these cases. The bus grant was later increased to 50 per cent and the grant specifications were subsequently amended and relaxed.

The main critics of the bus grant specifications were the operators who wanted to continue buying front-engined double-deckers, though there were fewer of these by then. The last AEC Regents, Guy Arabs and Leyland Titans for the British market were delivered in 1969; the previous year Northampton Corporation had received the last batch of Daimler CVG6s, the last truly traditional British double-deckers of the once familiar front engine/rear entrance type. Interestingly, these Roe-bodied CVG6s joined a fleet composed entirely of Roe-bodied CVG6s of varying ages.

The last British front-engined double-deckers were all for municipal operators and this was the main market. The Bristol Lodekka had last figured in Tilling Group orders for 1968 and the BET fleets had turned to rear-engined models or high-capacity single-deckers. The Scottish Bus Group had bought its last Lodekkas in 1967 and was ordering Bristol VRTs and Daimler Fleetlines to meet its double-deck requirements. SBG was a constant and vocal critic of rear-engined double-deckers — its Bristol VRTs were exchanged for National Bus Lodekkas by 1974 — but it was to play its part in an unexpected latter-day resurrection of the front-engine layout.

One other factor which undoubtedly played its part in the death of the front-engined double-decker was the formation of British Leyland, which faced many problems as it tried to weld together manufacturers who had been deadly rivals. Its main problems were on the private car side and much of BLMC's investment went towards improving this situation. The commercial vehicles were left rather to fend for themselves and it was hardly surprising that Leyland decided to rationalise its complex bus range and cancel out some of the inevitable duplication — hence the hasty demise of the front-engined double-deckers and the general acceptance, however reluctant, of the grant-preferred rear-engined types.

But if the bus grants were an important short-term result of the Transport Act, the emergence of the Passenger Transport Authorities, as the new conurbation bodies were designated, were of greater long-term significance. The first four PTAs were in busy urban areas where history had blurred formerly clear-cut boundaries, and where several municipal transport undertakings were serving large centres of population, sometimes on a joint basis, sometimes quite independently. The 1966 White Paper suggested that these new authorities should be created in those areas where it was felt necessary 'for the effective organisation and planning of public transport'. In practice, the first four PTAs were to be in the Birmingham, Manchester, Liverpool and Newcastle conurbations.

The PTAs were to be the policy-forming bodies, comprising local authority representatives and other local people. The day-to-day management was to be controlled by Passenger Transport Executives, each controlled by a Director General and a small group of specialist Directors.

On four month-apart vesting dates the new PTEs took over the existing municipal bus undertakings in their areas. The first, on 1 October 1969, was West Midlands PTE, combining the Birmingham, Walsall, West Bromwich and Wolverhampton municipalities; next was Selnec (South East Lancashire, North East Cheshire), combining Manchester with Ashton, Bolton, Bury, Leigh, Oldham, Ramsbottom, Rochdale, SHMD, Salford and Stockport; then came Merseyside PTE, an amalgam of

New liveries for nationalised coaches. *Below:* A Daimler Roadliner with Plaxton 47-seat body; although it is in the *Black & White* fleet, it is in the now-familiar all-white National coach livery. *Foot of page:* Scottish Bus Group introduced a blue/white livery for its Scotland-London services in 1976, and this is carried by one of the special 12metre Alexander-bodied coaches used on these services — this is an Eastern Scottish Bristol REMH 42-seater.

the Liverpool, Birkenhead and Wallasey fleets; last of the first four PTEs was Tyneside, consisting only of the physically separate Newcastle and South Shields undertakings.

Under the Transport Act the PTEs were charged to 'secure or promote the provision of a properly integrated and efficient system of public passenger transport', and this involved liaison with other operators in the area, including British Rail. At first though, it meant integrating municipal bus operators with very different backgrounds, very different outlooks and very different fleet sizes — including some of the largest fleets in the country. Selnec, the largest of the PTEs, inherited some 2,500 buses of many different

makes; the municipalities it encompassed all had highly individual views about the ideal vehicle. Leylands, inevitably in Lancashire, were predominant, but there were many Daimlers and even some representatives from AEC, Albion, Atkinson, Bedford, Bristol, Dennis and Guy. With such a mixed inheritance, Selnec started to develop standard vehicle types which would suit its conditions. Several of the former municipal fleets which passed to Selnec, notably Manchester, Bolton and Oldham, had worked hard to design really modern and well-considered double-deckers for their services, and some of the best points were incorporated into the prototype Selnec standard types which first appeared in 1971.

Selnec PTE chose a modern orange/white livery to replace the multitude of reds, greens and blues previously worn by its vehicles. The other PTEs stuck to liveries based on those formerly carried by the main constituents, so West Midlands buses carried Birmingham blue/cream, Tyneside carried Newcastle yellow/cream, and Liverpool area buses of Merseyside PTE carried Liverpool green. The Merseyside buses across the Mersey in the Wirral area of Cheshire were painted blue/cream.

The four original PTEs grew as they became established. Selnec acquired from NBC the services of North Western which ran within the Greater Manchester area, while the rest of this famous company was split between Crosville, Trent and National Travel. The unusual Selnec name was becoming increasingly familiar when, on local government reorganisation in April 1974, the PTE became the Greater Manchester PTE; the new Greater Manchester County included Wigan, and the municipal buses there passed into GMT control.

The West Midlands PTE acquired a large part of the Midland Red operation in 1973, the local services within the PTE area, while the boundary reshuffle in 1974 added the Coventry municipal fleet.

At Merseyside the boundary changes brought the Southport and St. Helens undertakings under PTE control. On Tyneside, the Sunderland Corporation bus fleet was acquired in 1974, when the PTE was named Tyne & Wear PTE. Here, as in other PTEs, local agreements have been reached with NBC and other operators; certain Northern General buses operating within the Tyne & Wear boundary, for instance, wear a yellow livery based on that of the PTE and there have been major service revisions.

Three new PTEs were added to the original four in 1973/74. The first, Greater

Below: **London Transport opted for the Daimler Fleetline as its standard double-deck model for the 1970s; these two early examples are in unrelieved all-red livery — later deliveries of LT Fleetlines were supplied with white relief, which helped the rather drab and uninspired appearance of these buses — compare them with the photo on page 105.** *Foot of page:* **London Country soon formulated its own vehicle policy, with deliveries like this 1973 Bristol LHS6L with ECW 35-seat body.**

Glasgow, which took over the former Glasgow Corporation Transport operation on 1 June 1973, was unique for several reasons; it is the only PTE in Scotland, is the only PTE based on just one undertaking and the only PTE with an underground railway, the vintage Subway system. Then in April 1974 the South Yorkshire and West Yorkshire PTEs were established. The South Yorkshire body took over the Doncaster, Rotherham and Sheffield municipalities, while West Yorkshire PTE took over Bradford, Halifax (with the related Calderdale JOC), Huddersfield and Leeds undertakings.

The new PTEs adopted distinctive liveries. South Yorkshire chose an unusual brown/cream, while Greater Glasgow and West Yorkshire plumped for a shade called Verona Green, though the livery applications are very different, and Glasgow also includes a strong yellow and added white relief. West Yorkshire uses a cream relief colour called Buttermilk, while Merseyside replaced the old Liverpool green with the Verona shade, relieved by Jonquil Yellow — a livery now applied to buses in all Divisions of the PTE.

Mergers and name-changes

The whole face of British municipal bus operation changed in the years from 1969 to 1975. With the formation of the PTEs, and Local Government reorganisation, the total number of British municipalities dropped from 91 to 51 in these six years. There were mergers and name-changes in April 1974 in England and Wales, while in May 1975 the three remaining Scottish municipalities passed into the control of the Regional Councils, the top-tier authorities, equivalent to the Counties south of the border.

Many familiar names disappeared during this period, as fleets merged and famous independent operators were acquired to help PTEs and NBC fleets to consolidate their position.

But the biggest upheaval was undoubtedly caused by the formation of National Bus Company, faced with the fusion of two very different groups of bus fleets. Both Tilling and BET went about things in their own highly individualistic ways. In some areas the BET and Tilling companies overlapped; in other fleets of one or other group reigned supreme. With their tramway origins, the BET companies could be found in many industrial areas, while Tilling fleets tended to serve the more rural parts of England and Wales. Inevitably there were exceptions, like the BET fleets in the predominantly rural south-east corner of England, but the pattern was there. The Tilling fleets held the less-populated areas — the extreme north of

England, both on the east and the west; the whole of East Anglia; north Wales; and the more distant parts of the West Country. The BET fleets were on Tyneside, around Manchester, Birmingham and the Potteries, in industrial Yorkshire and the South Wales valleys.

The 20,000 buses inherited by NBC were a mixed bunch, too. There was a wide selection of makes, layouts and styles from the BET fleets, intermixed with the orderly Bristol/ECW monopoly in the Tilling strongholds. Although BET had ideas about vehicle design, they were by no means as rigidly enforced as in the rival camp, where

Top: **The integral Leyland National model has become an increasingly familiar sight, in NBC, local authority and independent fleets. This 1975 example is shown in service with the independent Fishwick of Leyland.** *Above:* **Swedish-built Volvo chassis were bought by several British operators for coach work, like this version with Plaxton Panorama Elite body for St. Albans Travel.**

Two examples of the co-operation between Scania, in Sweden, and Metro-Cammell, in Britain. The single-deck Metro-Scania model is represented by this 1971 Leicester Corporation example (*top*). This was further developed as the double-deck Metropolitan (*above*) again shown in Leicester service.

develop and improve its express network, and since 1972 National coaches have been painted in a distinctive all-white livery with National symbol and fleetname in blue and red.

At the same time, new liveries were introduced for NBC stage carriage vehicles. Two standard shades, red and green, were adopted to replace the multitude of colours previously in use. The fleet colour, red or green, was applied in an all-over scheme to service buses, sometimes with a white relief band; dual-purpose vehicles received the local coach livery, with the fleet colour on the lower half and a white top. In all cases fleetnames are applied in a standard style, with the NBC 'double-N' logotype.

Scottish Bus Group, on the other hand, has jealously maintained the separate identities of its seven operating companies, though its one concession to a corporate identity was the introduction of a standard blue/white livery for the Scotland-London express coaches of four of its subsidiary fleets, featuring a prominent 'SCOTTISH' fleetname.

Otherwise the Group structure has changed little and the only major change on this bus side since the formation of the Scottish Transport Group has been the gradual absorption of the widespread MacBrayne bus empire, mainly into the Highland fleet, and the subsequent withdrawal from Islay, Harris and Mull, leaving Skye and Bute as the SBG's last island strongholds.

The mint with the hole

The changes of January 1969 were only a start. Exactly one year later the giant London Transport empire was split into two, corresponding with the old Central and Country Areas. On that day the London Transport Board was replaced by the new London Transport Executive, responsible to the Greater London Council, which assumed control for an area of about 630 square miles, mostly within a radius of 15 miles from Charing Cross, and roughly corresponding to the GLC area. The green Country and Green Line fleets passed to a new subsidiary of NBC, London Country Bus Services Ltd.

London Country inherited its fair share of problems. After several years as a poor relation to the red Central Area buses, the green Country Area fleet had become an elderly collection — RTs and RFs in the main, but with newer vehicles including Routemaster buses and coaches, and a growing fleet of Merlin/Swift variants. Fleet renewal was an obvious priority and the first new buses received after the split were LT-

the existence of tame chassis and body builders was the most important factor.

With 44 operating units, the organisation of NBC was of prime importance and initially England and Wales were divided into ten Regions, but a simpler structure was favoured. By 1972 the stage carriage companies were grouped into three Regions; Eastern, Southern and Western. A fourth arm of the NBC structure, the Central Activities Group, was formed to control express services and tours. Initially only the NBC all-coach fleets came under the new Group, but gradually the main coaching activities of all NBC companies — and consequently about 3,000 coaches — were brought into the control of National Travel, a subsidiary formed in 1973.

Organisation and marketing of coach services on a national basis allowed NBC to

style AEC Swifts. Leyland Atlantean double-deckers and AEC Reliance coaches were quickly ordered, and vehicles were diverted from other NBC subsidiaries — Daimler Fleetlines, Leyland Atlanteans and AEC Swifts.

The LT image was quickly abandoned and London Country soon adopted the guise of a typical NBC fleet though this was far from the case. London Country and its problems were treated as a special case by NBC, not least because of the unusual shape of its area; John Aldridge appositely described it as "a network that looked like the mint with the hole". Special buses, Metro-Scanias and Leyland Nationals, were bought for the experimental Superbus services in Stevenage; the Nationals were the first of a large fleet for London Country, buses and Green Line coaches. London Country and London Transport each chose ECW-bodied Bristol LHs for RF replacement, an interesting example of similar thinking (though the Country LHs pre-dated LT's by at least two years).

Even without a large part of its less remunerative services, London Transport's remit was a difficult one. The traffic conditions in the heart of London were steadily deteriorating and LT's resources were stretched to the limit. The problems with the large intake of single-deckers had disrupted the fleet replacement programme. A shorter variation of the unhapy Merlins had been ordered, a 33ft 5in bus based on the AEC Swift chassis, with the rear-mounted 8.2litre AH505 engine. The first 50 were one-door 42-seat buses classified SM, but the rest, 650 SMS buses, were two-door vehicles. All were delivered between 1970 and 1972, and proved more successful than their longer brothers; indeed in 1973 it was announced that the 36ft MB family would be sold prematurely. The Merlins and Swifts did allow LT to expand one-man operated services and after experiments with the Leyland Atlanteans, one-man double-deckers came to London.

When large orders were placed for new double-deckers, LT chose the Daimler Fleetline model and the first, with two-door Park Royal 68-seat bodywork, appeared in 1970. The new Fleetlines were fitted for one-man operation and were classified DMS. The first DMS vehicles entered service early in 1971 and have been followed by large quantities of similar vehicles, some with Metro-Cammell bodies.

With the DMS, LT proved what it had been saying all along: that operating conditions in London are uniquely arduous. The Fleetline, virtually bought 'off the peg', turned out to be mechanically less reliable

Above: **Bedford's mid-engined chassis proved popular for bus and coach work. This 10m YLT with Plaxton Supreme body was delivered in 1976 to Braybrooke of Mendlesham.** *Below:* **Ford's popular front-engined R192, with Willowbrook bus body, bought by Whyte's in 1970 for use on Heathrow Airport services.**

A Leyland Terrier with midi-size Sparshatt body, a type popular for staff transport.

London Merlins for sale after a short life — this advert appeared in the trade press in 1977.

than its made-to-measure predecessors. Added to this were problems with deliveries and a shortage of spare parts.

London also bought Fleetlines equipped for conventional two-man operation, classified DM, and the next new type of double-deck bus for LT was also designed for crew operation. This was an order for 164 of the Anglo-Swedish Metropolitan model, described later in this chapter. It was the double-deck equivalent of the Metro-Scania city bus, six of which were bought by LT in 1973 for experimental operation alongside six Leyland Nationals. These 12 buses represented modern thinking in city bus design, with fully-automatic transmission, air suspension, power-assisted steering and extra soundproofing.

One London innovation around this time was the appearance of the first overall advertising bus, for Silexene Paints, in 1969. This brightly-painted Routemaster was the first of many advert buses to appear in London, and eventually in many other parts of Britain. Faced with this novel form of mobile hoarding, advertisers and designers had a field-day and some really bizarre confections resulted.

Although LT had its large fleet of Merlins and Swifts, many had been bought as double-deck replacements. There was a pressing need for a shorter, smaller-capacity model to replace the dwindling fleet of RFs, AEC Regal IVs, dating from 1952-54. The eventual choice was the Bristol LH model, with ECW body, and deliveries started in 1976. Even smaller vehicles were the 20 Ford Transits delivered in 1972/73 at the request of the GLC, for one-man operated minibus routes in London suburbs, often on roads not previously served by buses.

The National unveiled

While London was experiencing single-deck problems, manufacturers and operators in the rest of Britain were anticipating the decline of the double-decker and increasing demand for high-capacity single-deck buses. The forecast was mistaken, as it turned out. In 1969 British Leyland and National Bus got together to form a new company, the Leyland National Co Ltd, to manufacture a completely new integral city bus at a new purpose-built plant at Workington. The project was inaugurated early in 1970 and later that year, at the London Commercial Show, the prototype National was unveiled. As introduced, the bus was available in 10.3m or 11.3m lengths, as a one-door or two-door bus, and in right- or left-hand drive versions. The rigid specification reflected the high degree of automation at the £8.5m Workington plant, for the National is built

on production line techniques learned from Leyland's experience in the private car industry.

The low-floor National, with rear-mounted Leyland 8.2 litre 510 turbocharged engine, quickly became a familiar sight in many parts of Britain; National Bus, inevitably, has been the main customer, but demand has gradually built up towards the 40 buses a week figure for which the factory was designed.

The concept of rigid standardisation has been abandoned to a certain extent. A £20,000 Business Commuter version appeared in 1972 and in the following year an intermediate length 10.9m version appeared, aimed mainly at the export market. Later in 1973 the Suburban Express, with flat floor and coach seats, made its debut and in 1974 the National was used as the basis for the Lifeliner, a fully-equipped casualty-clearing unit.

After a troublesome start, with more than its fair share of teething troubles the National has settled down to become a familiar part of British bus operation and, increasingly, can be found in many parts of the world. Although there are unlikely to be any major changes in the design of the National for some time, its development is ongoing and constant improvements are made in the light of operating experience. One option, important environmentally, is the quiet pack, first fitted to London Transport's experimental batch, and likely to become an important feature.

The arrival of the National prompted a certain amount of activity among other builders. One side-effect was Leyland's decision to discontinue production of competing chassis in its own range, hence the relatively early demise of the Bristol RE and Leyland Panther ranges. This in turn affected the independent bodybuilders, who saw the source of separate chassis drying up in favour of the integral National. Some counteracted this by specialising in double-deckers, though a similar situation was due to affect the double-deck market. Metro-Cammell entered an agreement with the Swedish bus and truck builders Scania, to build a model for the British single-deck market, the Metro-Scania, based on the Scania BR111 model, but assembled in Birmingham.

The first Metro-Scanias appeared in 1969, integral city buses available in 10m and 11m lengths, with rear-mounted Scania 11litre engines and fully-automatic transmission. This sophisticated model enjoyed a certain success, entering service with a number of municipal and PTE fleets, and even with London Country, London Transport and the

Winchester independent King Alfred. With National Bus heavily committed to the National, though, Metro-Cammell found the single-deck market restricted and chose to concentrate on a double-decker with Scania units. There was one coach aimed at the British market, based on the Scania CR145 model, but its advanced specification — with 14.2litre V8 engine, air suspension and power-assisted steering — meant a high price-tag and it created little interest.

Seddon introduced a rear-engined bus chassis in 1969, the RU model with Gardner 6HLX engine, and although it enjoyed a certain success, it had a relatively short life on the British market. Seddon became more involved in the bus market at this time and offered several variations on its Pennine chassis range, with front, rear and underfloor-mounted engines. The most novel was the Seddon Midi, a 6.5m bus with Pennine Coachcraft body built on a Pennine IV 236 chassis. This useful little 25-seat bus was fitted with the 3.86litre Perkins 4.236 engine, driving through a five-speed synchromesh gearbox, though later versions for Greater Manchester PTE had Allison fully-automatic transmission.

A bigger Seddon, the Pennine VII, appeared in 1973, and was developed in conjunction with the Scottish Bus Group. It was a traditional heavy-duty underfloor-engined model suitable for 11m or 12m bodies, and combined a number of well-tried components like the Gardner 6HLXB engine, ZF four-speed gearbox and Lipe-Rollway twin-plate clutch. The Scottish Group companies have bought this chassis in large quantities and other operators have specified it for coach work.

During the early 1970s, imported cars and trucks were taking an increasingly large slice of the British market and it was inevitable that bus builders should attempt to follow suit. Scania's involvement with Metro-Cammell has already been described, and Swedish rival Volvo has made the most concentrated attack, picking up some useful sales in Britain for its 11m and 12m B58 coach chassis. This model was first imported in 1972 and features an underfloor-mounted 9.6litre engine. At the same time the B59 rear-engined city bus chassis was introduced to Britain, but although this highly-sophisticated bus was enthusiastically received — a *Motor Transport* tester described it as 'one of the most impressive public service vehicles I have ever handled' — no sales were made.

On a smaller scale, full-size chassis have been imported by Mercedes-Benz and DAF and it seems likely that there will be others, particularly following Britain's entry into the Common Market.

But the British manufacturers continued to dominate the home market, with a well-tried range of models. British Leyland had the steadily-selling underfloor-engined chassis, the AEC Reliance, Bristol LH and Leyland Leopard. The LH, favoured by NBC and London Transport as a lightweight 9.5m service bus, also found a market in its LHS form as the basis for short-length bus and coach bodies.

The Reliance, and particularly the Leopard, continued to sell steadily as heavyweight coach chassis. National Travel and Scottish Bus Group, and important independents like Barton, Grey Green and Wallace Arnold, chose the Leopard as a

The Volvo Ailsa double-decker marked a return to the front-engined layout that was welcomed in some circles. Many of the Ailsas built have had Alexander bodies of the style shown on this 1976 example for the Doncaster area independent operator Premier, Stainforth.

103

standard coach model, while the Scottish fleets, among others, also specified Leopard buses. Since 1968 a proportion of the Reliance and Leopard coach chassis has been built to the 12m overall length, legalised at that time, but 11m remains the most popular size.

Bedford and Ford retained their dominant position in the lightweight coach market and increasingly they were specified for rural bus duties by independents, municipalities and nationalised fleets. Bedford replaced its 10m VAM model in 1970 with the YRQ, with a centrally-mounted vertical underfloor engine, and this was followed by the 11m YRT in 1972; these were replaced by the bigger-engined YLQ and YMT chassis in 1975. Ford, on the other hand, stuck to the front-engined R1014 and R1114 models, improved versions of chassis that had first appeared in the mid-1960s.

The growth of special services requiring smaller buses created a market for mini and midi size vehicles. In addition to the van-based minibuses like the Bedford CF, Commer PB and Ford Transit, and the bigger Ford A, Leyland Terrier and Mercedes L406D, there were specially-developed integral midibuses from coachbuilders like Alexander and Marshall.

Hobson's Choice?

There was very little choice where double-deckers were concerned. For some time only British Leyland's three-model range, Bristol VR/Daimler Fleetline/Leyland Atlantean, was available and there were complaints from operators that they were not available enough. While BLMC poured its investment cash into the private car divisions, the normally profitable commercial vehicle side was struggling to maintain deliveries of new chassis and spare parts. And there was an increasing undercurrent of dissatisfaction with the reliability of the rear-engined designs compared with the now-discontinued front-engined models.

Leyland struggled on, though. The Leyland 680 engine was offered in the Daimler Fleetline — a particularly valuable option for a period when Gardner engines were in short supply. Then there was the AN68 Atlantean, a vastly improved version of the 14-year old PDR series, introduced in 1972.

These efforts did not please every operator. In 1972 Northern General unveiled two remarkable confections, the Tynesider and the Wearsider. With a successful fleet of Routemasters, Northern was looking for a way of converting these for one-man operation. The Tynesider was the first step towards this, a Leyland PD3 Titan heavily

rebuilt as a normal control vehicle, with the driver alongside the forward entrance, behind a Routemaster-type 'snout'. The next stage was the conversion of an accident-damaged Routemaster in a similar fashion, the Wearsider, but there have been no more of these remarkable rebuilds.

Apart from Northern General's efforts, double-deckers started to look much more similar around this time, mainly following the introduction of a crisp new standard design from Park Royal-Roe in 1969. This was quickly adopted by most of the PTEs, by NBC for Atlantean chassis, and even by London Transport — probably the first time that most of the major operators in England have operated similar-looking buses. The design was produced, with modifications, by Park Royal and Roe, and by Metro-Cammell, Northern Counties and Willowbrook, all in the interests of standardisation.

The Scottish Bus Group continued to favour the front-engined double-decker, and acted in an advisory capacity in the development of a new model, the Ailsa. The Scottish-based Ailsa Trucks group had successfully imported Volvo trucks for some years, and the Ailsa bus featured a Volvo engine. This was the 6.7litre TD70 unit, a compact turbocharged engine which fitted neatly beside the driving position to allow a normal entrance on the front overhang.

The Volvo Ailsa was supplied as an underframe and Alexander built an integrated body structure on many of the early examples, following its introduction in 1973.

Leyland's monopoly was further challenged the same year by the appearance of yet another British/Swedish collaboration, the Metropolitan. This was essentially a double-deck version of the Metro-Scania city bus, and like the Ailsa was ordered in reasonable numbers by PTE and municipal fleets, though there were signs of a falling-off in demand as Leyland's future plans became clearer. It was known that an advanced double-deck model was in development, and that it could eventually replace the VR/Fleetline/Atlantean trio.

The replacement was to be a gradual one, though, with the Fleetline disappearing first. After 7,000-plus chassis Fleetline production had transferred from Coventry to Leyland and in 1976 even adopted the Leyland name. The demand for a Gardner-engined successor prompted Foden and Dennis to re-enter the double-deck market with new rear-engined models in 1976 and 1977.

The success of the AN68 Atlantean has guaranteed a stay of execution, while the improvements made to Bristol's VRT model

"They've made some pretty extensive cuts on this route."

Variations on a standard theme. The double-deck body style first introduced by Park Royal in 1969 has been widely imitated, and can be seen throughout the country with detail differences. *Left:* **Two Park Royal products, for London Transport on Fleetline chassis, and for Ribble on Atlantean.** *Below left:* **Park Royal's associate Roe built this Atlantean for Ipswich Borough Transport.** *Bottom:* **The Northern Counties version, on Fleetline chassis, for Greater Manchester Transport.**

in 1974 have ensured that it will retain its place in the model lists for some time to come. The Mark 3 version of the VRT features a Leyland 510 engine as an option to the Gardner units normally fitted, totally encapsulated to achieve an external noise level of 80dB(A) — well within the Government-proposed legislation of 85-86dB(A).

A glimpse of the future

The bus which could eventually replace these chassis appeared late in 1975, when details of the Leyland B15 were revealed. Like the existing Leyland double-deckers it is rear-engined; in Leyland's words 'the location of the mechanical units takes second place to the needs of the fare-paying passengers and driver'. The engine is the TL11, a turbo-charged version of the Leyland 680 series, rated at 170bhp, though a Gardner engine can be fitted instead. The production version of the B15, introduced in 1977, revives the type-name Titan, and is designated TN15.

From the driver's viewpoint, ease of control has been possible without sacrificing sensitivity. Power-assisted steering is fitted and a fully-automatic gearbox is standard, with a friction retarder integral with the transmission. A power hydraulic braking system is provided.

The new Titan is a highly-standardised design, available only in one body size, 9.5m × 2.5m, and only as a 4.4m normal height bus. Leyland intended the Bristol VRT to satisfy the decreasing demand for low-height vehicles.

The Titan's integral construction allows a low entrance step height, and saloon heights on both decks are more generous than normal. One-door and two-door buses will be available, and extensive Leyland research into human factors is reflected in the design and layout of the entrance and exit areas.

The Titan can carry 70-75 seated passengers and around 20 standees if required. The independent front suspension is by a combination of torsion bars and self-levelling

air suspension, while full self-levelling air suspension is provided at the rear.

Initial reaction to the Titan was uncharacteristically enthusiastic, and Leyland showed a commendable degree of care in the introduction of the model. The Bristol VR and Leyland National demonstrated the folly of rushing designs into production without adequate service proving, and their early reputation still lingers on.

The first B15 entered service with London Transport in 1976, on an experimental basis, and it may be that this advanced model will

The models which were standard purchases for many National Bus fleets in the mid-1970s, photographed in United Counties service at Luton. These two, a Bristol/ECW VRT and a Leyland National, were new in 1973.

suit LT's exacting requirements. There was a suggestion at one stage that LT might even assemble B15s at its Aldenham Works, but full-scale production was due to switch to the AEC factory at Southall, London, birthplace of many LT buses.

The gradual acceptance of integral vehicles has caused problems for the old-established bodybuilders outside the Leyland empire. Some have diversified. Alexander has built many Ailsas and has the integral S-type midibus; East Lancs has built coach bodies; Metro-Cammell linked with Scania to build the Metropolitan models and has further double-deck plans in hand with the Gardner or Rolls-Royce engined Metrobus. Northern Counties became involved in the Foden double-deck market. All of these builders had relied heavily on the lucrative double-deck market, increasingly so as the single-deck bus market dried up. The other major coachbuilders, Duple, Plaxton and Willow-brook have specialised in luxury coaches for many years and also build for the lightweight bus market.

The three builders under Leyland control, Eastern Coach Works, Park Royal and Roe, would seem to have an assured future. ECW will presumably still be required to build on Bristol LH and VR chassis for NBC, and on the proposed low-height underframe version of the Titan.

With the Titan, the VRT, and their competitors, it is tempting to wonder just who is going to buy them all. The Confederation of British Road Passenger Transport has produced forecasts of vehicle requirements for a 16-year period and anticipates a sharp drop in double-deck demand in the early 1980s. Demand, it prophesied, would be past its peak by 1980,

when all of the new designs should be in full production and the demand then could be falling below the normal combined output of Leyland, Ailsa and Metro-Cammell, without taking the Dennis and Foden — and any others — into account.

Alternative sources
All of this assumes that the diesel-engined bus will still predominate. For years the boffins had been busy predicting the problems the world would face when the energy crunch eventually came. Suddenly at the end of 1973 their gloomy forebodings proved dramatically accurate. Suddenly oil was in short supply and costing more each day, and the alternatives became more attractive.

The Americans revived the steam bus. Faced with the near-perpetual Los Angeles smog, the US Government embarked on a costly exercise which produced three steam buses. Externally there was little to distinguish them from their diesel brothers, particularly as they were driven by diesel oil. They were clean and performed well, but they used more fuel than their contemporaries and defeated part of the object of this particular exercise.

Electric power probably had most in its favour, though we have seen how British operators abandoned first the tramcar and then the trolleybus. Britain's final trolleybus system closed down in March 1972 when the Bradford system was abandoned; ironically, that same month, only nine miles away at Leeds, the first of a number of experimental battery buses entered service. The trial, sponsored by the Department of Trade and Industry, involved small buses built by Crompton Electricars on converted BLMC truck chassis and bodied by Willowbrook. These electric buses were used in various towns in Britain and were fairly successful. Greater Manchester PTE took the idea a couple of stages further with the Silent Rider project, a full-size Seddon/Chloride bus to be used at peak hours and recharged in between, and a Lucas electric version of the Seddon midibuses already operating on the busy Manchester Centreline service.

The problems with electric buses include the size and weight of batteries necessary, the limited mileage range and the slower acceleration, but many of the big manufacturers in Britain and on the Continent have projects in hand which may overcome these. A Leyland National converted for experimental use tows its batteries in a separate trailer, and this may be one answer to the difficulties with size, weight and recharging time.

Some of the Continental manufacturers have also experimented with gas buses, using liquefied petroleum gas(lpg). In Britain the Teesside undertaking introduced a Daimler Fleetline fitted with a Rolls-Royce engine converted to run on lpg, and London Transport has also conducted experiments.

A further resurgence of interest in electric power is the Tyne & Wear Metro, a light railway system that will, to all intents and purposes, be the equivalent of the modern tramway systems on the Continent. And there is, of course, the famous Blackpool seafront tramway, based on the long route from Fleetwood to Squires Gate, and operated by a mixed fleet, including some smart single-deckers rebuilt as one-man vehicles.

The energy crisis is only one of the problems facing the bus industry in recent years. There has been the rise in car ownership and the consequent fall in passenger figures, delays in vehicle and spare parts deliveries, the dramatic rise in all costs, changes in drivers' hours which have resulted in less flexibility, service unreliability through the lack of suitable vehicles or staff, or both — the list is seemingly endless.

But the picture is not as black as all this might suggest. The bus industry has not been content simply to sit back and let this happen, and has been conducting experiments to discover if the traditional concept of bus services developed mainly over the past half-century is still relevant to today's needs.

Many of these services were designed to serve long-established towns and cities, and the growth of new overspill towns since World War II has given busmen an opportunity to test new approaches. At Stevenage, encouraged by the Development

Corporation and the Government, London Country has developed the successful Superbus network. The first Superbus vehicles, painted in an eye-catching yellow/blue livery, appeared in 1971, part of a widely-publicised campaign to win passengers back to the buses. Services were revitalised, with increased frequencies and lowered fares, and modern vehicles, including Leyland Nationals and Metro-Scanias, were used. On the first Superbus service traffic has more than doubled — an illustration that a high standard of public

Top: **The end of an era — Britain's last trolleybus on its final journey from Bradford Town Hall to Thornton terminus in March 1972. The vehicle was a Sunbeam F4 which had been new in 1948 to Mexborough & Swinton as a single-decker, but received this East Lancs 66-seat body after acquisition by Bradford in 1962.** *Above:* **A newer form of electric traction — Greater Manchester's 1973 Silent Rider, a Chloride battery-powered Seddon 43-seater.**

A glimpse of the future — a prototype Metro-Cammell unit on the Tyne & Wear Metro test track.

bus. A variation is the frequent city centre service, providing a useful link during business hours for short-distance passengers; these usually have a single flat fare, but Nottingham Transport has carried things to a logical conclusion with its two Central Area Free Services.

Small, but useful

The layman who advocates minibuses as the answer to transport problems usually forgets that operating costs, and particularly the wages of the driver, do not decrease in proportion to the size of the vehicle. Added to this, the minibus is basically inflexible when faced with peak loads, and a lightly-loaded 45-seater which has the capacity when required is probably a more economical proposition. This is not to say that the minibus has no real future in public transport. In many cases, where smaller vehicles are essential or where the load is never likely to exceed the capacity, the minibus has an important role to play; in many cases it is the only way that any form of service can be provided.

In urban areas, smaller buses in both mini and midi size ranges have appeared increasingly on dial-a-ride and similar services. Passengers in some areas can phone a central control point to request transport into town and the driver will be contacted to arrange a pick up at the most convenient point — often the caller's front door. There is normally a basic route, with some form of timetable and fixed stops for those without phones, and the driver diverts to pick up and set down passengers as near to their homes as possible. These services operate under a variety of names and often serve residential suburbs which do not otherwise have a bus service.

Minibuses are also used on some of the city centre shoppers services, in some cases using pedestrian areas, but two more unusual uses are worth mentioning.

The first, the postbus, appeared experimentally in 1968, a BMC minibus which carried passengers as well as mail on a rural route in East Lothian. Four years later a postbus service on Skye marked the start of a fast-growing system operated by the Scottish Postal Board. Gradually, other services were started by the Post Office in more remote parts of the Scottish mainland and islands, and in parts of England and Wales as well.

Scotland's 50th postbus was launched in 1975 and the numbers grow annually, in some cases taking over services from established operators. The Dodge PB 11-seat minibus is the most popular vehicle for this type of service, and the driver not

service can keep the cars away.

At the Cheshire new town of Runcorn, the approach has been quite different. Here a 12-mile exclusive busway was built into the road network, allowing a rapid transit system in a basic figure-eight, but ensuring that no home is more than five minutes from a bus stop. The Crosville single-deck buses used can achieve an average running speed of 20mph, and the Runcorn Busway is the natural extension of the bus priority schemes which are now familiar in most towns and cities. The first bus lanes were in London, allowing service buses to avoid traffic snarl-ups at busy junctions, and the idea was extended to provide bus lanes running against the normal traffic-flow, thus avoiding lengthy and time-consuming one-way systems.

Park-and-ride services have been tried in many centres as an attempt to keep cars out of town and city centres by encouraging drivers to park at suburban car parks and travel into shopping or business areas by only collects and delivers mail, but also essential supplies; the postbus has become an important part of life in many isolated rural areas, a highly practical solution to at least some of the transport problems.

A quite different approach is the village bus, an experimental type of service first introduced in 1975. Its aim is to provide a self-help bus service for communities which would normally be too small to support a conventional service. Eastern Counties provided a 12-seat Ford Transit minibus for six Norfolk villages, where residents share the responsibility for their own public transport. The locals provide a team of volunteer drivers and handle normal operation, though Eastern Counties and Norfolk County Council, the joint sponsors, retain overall control.

The village bus mainly provides connections with rail and bus services to larger towns, and can be used for other purposes under imposed guidelines. The County Council backs the service financially, but the costs are much less than for a service using full-size buses, a situation which would never have been considered.

With all these new ideas and many more to come, the bus industry is clearly determined to ride out the problems and face the future with confidence. In these difficult times, no bus operator can really afford to be too backward-looking, but so much has happened to the motor bus in its relatively short history that laid the foundations for the system we know today, and the lessons of the past are often a useful pointer to the future.

The continued interest shown by many thousands of people in Britain in the history of the industry is reflected in the dramatic growth in bus preservation during the past two decades. There must now be literally thousands of old buses throughout the country in various stages of restoration and many of them can be seen at the multitude of rallies held during the summer months. The most dramatic sight is probably the annual Trans-Pennine Run, where many beautifully-preserved buses make the sometimes arduous journey from Manchester across to Harrogate.

London Transport, while it was still London General, led the way in ensuring that representative vehicles were set aside for preservation and started amassing a priceless collection which now ranges from 19th century horse buses through to the diesel-engined double-deckers of the 1930s. In 1973 the London Transport Collection moved to Syon Park, and this excellent museum is an invaluable reminder of the rapid development of the bus and of the

Two examples of the modern thinking in the bus industry. *Top:* The driver's eye view of the Runcorn Busway as two Crosville Pennine-bodied Seddon RUs pass each other. *Above:* The cover of a leaflet announcing the London Country Stevenage Superbus services.

The past fondly remembered — a 1943 Weymann-bodied utility Guy Arab II formerly in the Swindon Corporation fleet, and now lovingly preserved. It was one of the many entrants in the 1976 Trans-Pennine Run from Manchester to Harrogate.

The postbus fast became a feature of rural life in several parts of Britain, particularly in Scotland where the growing postbus network has provided vital connections for otherwise isolated communities. This Commer PB2500 is seen between Alligin and Kinlochewe in Scotland's Highland Region.

Right: The first of the village buses jointly sponsored by National Bus and Norfolk County Council. It is a Ford Transit / Deansgate 12-seater. *Below:* One of several special city centre services using midi-size buses, the West Midlands PTE Centrebus service in Birmingham was introduced with 19-seat Commer KCFs, one of which is seen here in a pedestrian precinct.

important part that London played in its early history.

Back in favour

The 1968 Transport Act was a sign that the bus was returning to official favour. With increasing pressure from environmentalists came the slow realisation that the bus was an economical and efficient load-mover. Other factors were the economic problems of the 1970s and the threat to the world's oil supplies.

A further indication of the Government's concern was the publication in 1976 of the consultation document *Transport Policy*, which concluded:

'It goes without saying (or rather it often goes with saying but without doing) that we want an efficient transport system in the interests of economic growth, export competitiveness and consumer satisfaction; indeed we need a much more efficient system than we have today'.

While it accepted the inevitable increase in car ownership, it also saw the need for a good basic public transport network, and a higher priority for essential bus services. It continued:

'Each major mode of transport — road, rail and bus — has its own characteristics and advantages. We must use our extensive and often under-praised transport system to the best advantage and ensure that each mode does the job for which it is best suited.'

These views were reinforced by the Transport White Paper in 1977, which promised the bus industry "an assured future".

All of these developments and proposals show a healthy concern for the future of the bus industry. Although its once strong position has been eroded by the growth in private car ownership, buses still account for more than 12 per cent of all travel in Britain. A total of 7.7billion bus journeys were made in 1974, in spite of the fact that 55 per cent of all households now own private cars, a figure which rises to 70 per cent in rural areas.

An estimated total of 217,500 were employed in road passenger transport in Britain, helping to run around 75,000 vehicles. London Transport, with more than 6,800 buses, remains the biggest individual operator, with the NBC group amassing 20,000-plus vehicles, Scottish Bus Group 4,300, the six PTEs 11,200, the 54 local authority fleets 6,200 and private operators around 25,500.

As we enter the last quarter of the 20th century, it is intriguing to speculate on the future of bus design, but crystal ball-gazing can be a dangerous pastime and this book should be more concerned with the past and present than with the future. Today's designs have reached such a level of sophistication that it is difficult to see how they could be improved, yet they probably said the same thing about the first Milnes-Daimler, or Leyland Lion, or four-wheel-drive Gilford, or AEC Routemaster, or Daimler Fleetline or Bristol RE. This is a good thing, for it demonstrates the constant development of the motor bus and it is reassuring to discover how difficult it is to please bus operators. No sooner had the prototype Leyland B15 double-decker entered experimental service with London Transport in 1976, than LT announced that it was working on a successor for the mid-1980s, which would offer a 'new dimension in passenger comfort, with even lower step heights'. The sentiments are laudable — and, over the last 80 years, increasingly familiar. As familiar, in fact, as the British motor bus.

The posters proclaim that Leyland's advanced B15 is 'London's Bus of Tomorrow', at a time before final production details of the Titan were known.

Bibliography

My references for this book have largely been the books and magazines I have read over the years, so it is to the authors, editors and contributors of these that I must extend my thanks.

The magazines which have been — and, indeed, continue to be — particularly valuable are the weekly *Commerical Motor* and *Motor Transport*, the monthly *Buses* and *Coaching Journal*, and *The Omnibus Magazine* and *Old Motor*. The books are greater in number and can all be recommended for further reading.

Taking company histories first, there are the two London Transport publications *The Story of the London Bus* and *The London Motor Bus*, while *The Southdown Story 1915-1965* also proved useful. Independently-published company histories which produced much valuable reference material were *History of Royal Blue Express Services* and *Hants & Dorset Motor Services*, the story of the Tilling family *Kings of the Highway*, and Clem Preece's reminiscences *Wheels to the West*.

Books dealing with the manufacturing side are fewer in number, but *The Leyland Papers* can be recommended as a fascinating insight into big business.

The early history of the bus is dealt with in Charles E Lee's twin booklets *The Horse Bus as a Vehicle* and *The Early Motor Bus*, and in *Buses and Trolleybuses before 1919*, and other useful publications dealing with later periods were *London Independent Bus Operators 1922-1933* and *British Double-Deckers since 1942*.

Two tramway books worth reading are *The Golden Age of Tramways* and *Tramway Twilight*, and trolleybuses are well covered in *Trolleybus Trails* and *History of the British Trolleybus*.

Over the years the Omnibus Society has produced publications which cover all aspects of the bus industry, and I found *The Rise and Decline of the Railway Bus*, *London Buses in Wartime* and *Extended Tours by Motor Coach* particularly useful.

Other Ian Allan books which provided references were *Buses Annual* over the years, my own anthology *Bus Stop*, and books in the *Buses in Camera* series.